DIVE GUIDE
MALTA, COMINO AND GOZO

OVER 80 TOP DIVE AND SNORKEL SITES

**LESLEY ORSON WOOD
AND LAWSON WOOD**

Foreword by the Minister for Tourism and Culture, Malta
Series Consultant: Nick Hanna

NEW HOLLAND

Lawson Wood has many years' experience as a diver and is one of the world's leading underwater photographers. A sports massage therapist by profession, Lesley Orson Wood has played a pivotal role in Lawson's previous books, as well as contributing her own articles to international dive magazines.

This second edition first published in the United Kingdom in 2006 by
New Holland Publishers (UK) Ltd
London • Cape Town • Sydney • Auckland
www.newhollandpublishers.com

Garfield House	80 McKenzie Street	Unit 4, 14 Aquatic Drive	Unit 1A, 218 Lake Road
86–88 Edgware Road	Cape Town 8001	Frenchs Forest, NSW 2086	Northcote, Auckland
London W2 2EA UK	South Africa	Australia	New Zealand

10 9 8 7 6 5 4 3 2 1
First published in 1999

Copyright © 2006 in text: Lesley Orson Wood and Lawson Wood
Copyright © 2006 in The Marine Environment (by Lawson Wood): New Holland Publishers (UK) Ltd
Copyright © 2006 in Underwater Photography (by Lawson Wood): New Holland Publishers (UK) Ltd
Copyright © 1999 in Health and Safety: New Holland Publishers (UK) Ltd
Copyright © 2006 in photographs: Lesley Orson Wood and Lawson Wood (except individual photographers as credited below)
Copyright © 2006 in artwork and cartography: New Holland Publishers (UK) Ltd
Copyright © 1999, 2006: New Holland Publishers (UK) Ltd

All rights reserved. No part of this publication may be reproduced, stored in a retrieval system or transmitted, in any form or by any means, electronic, mechanical, photocopying, recording or otherwise, without the prior written permission of the publishers and copyright holders.

ISBN 1 84330 942 4

Project development: Charlotte Parry-Crooke
Series editors: Pete Duncan, Kate Michell
Assistant editor: Kate Parker
Copy editor: Brigitte Lee
Proofreader: Paul Barnett
Design concept: Philip Mann, ACE Ltd
Design: Behram Kapadia
Cartography: ML Design
Production: Joan Woodroffe

Reproduction by Hirt and Carter, South Africa
Printed and bound in Singapore by Tien Wah Press (Pte) Ltd

Photographic Acknowledgements
All photographs taken by Lesley Orson Wood and Lawson Wood except for the following:
page 42: Natural History Museum, Malta; page 43: Jeff Rotman/BBC Natural History Unit

Front cover: *The seahorse Hippocampus ramulosus has a crest from head to dorsal fin.*
Spine: *A white-tufted worm (Protula tubularia) extends itself on a submarine wall.*
Back cover: *The Beaufighter 'N', off St Julian's Point.*
Title page: *The anchor from the Rozi (Malta, Site 26) is now encrusted in sponges and algae.*
Contents page: *A rocky reef off Cirkewwa on Malta teems with small chromis and colourful starfish.*
Foreword: *Rising high above central Malta is the ancient walled city of Mdina.*

Although the author and publisher have made every effort to ensure that the information in this book was correct at the time of going to press, they accept no responsibility for any loss, injury or inconvenience sustained by any person using this book.

AUTHORS' ACKNOWLEDGEMENTS

This book was made possible with the help of the Malta Tourist Office in Malta and in the UK, who supported the project from its inception. Their professionalism and dedication are gratefully acknowledged, with special thanks to Naala Buckland for her superb organization, Valerie Carre, Alexandra Valletta, Jeffrey Cutajar and Major Alfred Cassar Reynaud.

Particular thanks go to: Francis Zammit Dimech, Minister of Tourism and Culture; Karmenu Vella, Maltese High Commissioner in London; the University of Malta; Bet Bithrey, a special friend who gives far more than she receives; Air Malta; Joe Vella Gaffiero, Director of the Natural History Museum; Anthony Rogers; Simon and Hermine Sammut; Doris Cusens, an extraordinary Maltese guide who taught us about the other side of Malta, and her husband Tom, who helped with translations; Andy Probert, Paul Brewer, Dolores and Aquaventure Ltd; Melovan Galea of Meldives Malta; Tony Lautier and Tony's Dive Services, Comino; Joseph Messina and Joseph Saliba at the Comino Hotel; Ian Hulland and the Sharks, Malta BSAC Branch 1818; Kim Harrison, a superb videographer and mine of information; Victor J. Borg, who with his daughter Monica organized our accommodation on Gozo at the Ta' Cenc, Cornucopia and St Patrick's hotels (a special thanks); John Cutajar at Ta' Cenc; George Zammit Briffa, General Manager of Captain Morgan Cruises, for our helicopter flight; Gozo Channel Company for our ferry transfers; Westminster Car Hire for rental vehicles; Grand Hotel Mercure Selmun Palace; Eden Beach Hotel; Suncrest Hotel; Gillieru Harbour Hotel; Lewis at Dive Systems; Pierre for getting us onto the Bristol Blenheim; Edward Camilleri at Underwaterworld; Europcar; Grand Hotel Mercure San Antonio; Vince from Nature Trust Malta; Victoria Hotel, Sliema; Sharon Camilleri; Simon Theuma of Diverse Sea and my good friend Ned Middleton for his exemplary research into the many shipwrecks around the islands. Further information can also be gleaned from the Malta Marine Foundation, 2 Airways House, High Street, Sliema, Malta; tel (356) 99425351; e-mail: info@marinefoundation.org.

Specific mention must be made of the unswerving help and professionalism offered to both the authors by Mark Busuttil and all the members of St Andrew's Divers Cove at Xlendi on Gozo, and Agnes Upton and the staff of Maltaqua at StPauls on Malta. Both organisations are incredibly helpful, supportive and extremely professional in all aspects of diver training and safety.

PUBLISHERS' ACKNOWLEDGEMENTS

The publishers gratefully acknowledge the generous assistance during the compilation of this book of the following: Nick Hanna for his involvement in developing the series and consulting throughout and Dr Elizabeth M. Wood for acting as Marine Biological Consultant and contributing to The Marine Environment.

PHOTOGRAPHY

The authors' photographs were taken using the Nikonos V, Nikon D100, Nikon F-801, Nikon F-90, Ricoh 301 and the Fuji F-810. Lenses used on the amphibious Nikonos system were 35mm, 15mm and 12mm. The lenses used for the housed Nikons were 10.5mm, 14mm, 60mm, 105mm, 20-40mm zoom, 28-200mm zoom, 70-300mm zoom. Housing manufacture was by Subal and Sea & Sea.

Electronic flash was used in virtually all of the underwater photographs and these were only supplied by Sea & Sea Ltd from Paignton, Devon, UK and Japan. These were the YS30 Duo, YS60, YS90 Duo, TS120 Duo, YS300 and the YS350. Additional lighting was supplied by Niterider. Film stock was Fujichrome Velvia and Provia supplied by Calumet in Edinburgh and Fuji UK. Film processing was done by Eastern at Musselburgh. Latterly, all new photographs were taken digitally.

Diving equipment was supplied by Scubapro, except the fins which were supplied by our great friend and genius Bob Evans of Force Fin.

CONTENTS

Foreword

Malta's strategic position in the centre of the Mediterranean, together with its clear and clean seas, make it an ideal destination for divers. Underwater diving is one of Malta's niche markets attracting over 50,000 visitors to our islands every year.

Malta's dive sites, diving schools and diving centres, guaranteed safety standards and protection of the sea together with its flora and fauna form the necessary infrastructure for the underwater diving sector.

Standards within this sector are enhancing Malta's image as a diver's mecca with underwater divers coming from Northern European countries all the year round since sea temperatures in Malta never drop below 13°C, with a climate and duration of sunshine which in winter is similar to an average North European summer.

On behalf of the people and Government of Malta it is my pleasure to invite you to visit our islands, to live seven thousand years of civilisation and to see for yourself the leisure attractions which our islands offer throughout the year.

FRANCIS ZAMMIT DIMECH
Minister for Tourism and Culture, Malta

How to Use this Book

THE REGIONS
The dive sites included in this book are divided into three islands: Malta, Comino and Gozo. Regional introductions describe the key characteristics and features of each island and provide background information on climate, the environment, points of interest, and advantages and disadvantages of diving in the locality.

THE MAPS
Maps are included throughout each regional section to identify the location of the dive sites described and to provide other useful information for divers and snorkellers. Although certain reefs are indicated, the maps do not set out to provide detailed nautical information, such as exact reef contours. In general the maps show: the locations of the dive sites, indicated by white numbers in red boxes corresponding to those placed at the start of each dive site description; the locations of key access points to the sites (ports, beach resorts and so on); reefs and wrecks. Each site description gives details of how to access the dive site. (Note: the border round the maps is not a scale bar.)

MAP LEGEND

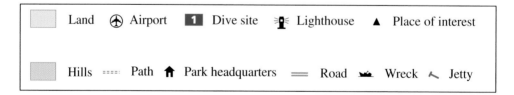

| | Land | ✈ Airport | ▣ Dive site | Lighthouse | ▲ Place of interest |
| Hills | ⋯ Path | Park headquarters | Road | Wreck | Jetty |

THE DIVE SITE DESCRIPTIONS
Within the geographical sections are the descriptions of each region's premier dive sites. Each site description starts with a number (to enable the site to be located on the corresponding map), a star-rating and a selection of key symbols, as shown opposite.

Crucial practical details (on location, access, conditions, typical visibility and minimum and maximum depths) precede the description of the site, its marine life, and special points of interest. In these entries, 'typical visibility' assumes good conditions.

THE STAR-RATING SYSTEM

Each site has been awarded a star-rating, with a maximum of five red stars for diving and five blue stars for snorkelling.

Diving		Snorkelling	
★★★★★	**first class**	★★★★★	**first class**
★★★★	**highly recommended**	★★★★	**highly recommended**
★★★	**good**	★★★	**good**
★★	**average**	★★	**average**
★	**poor**	★	**poor**

THE SYMBOLS

The symbols placed at the start of each site description provide a quick reference to crucial information pertinent to individual sites.

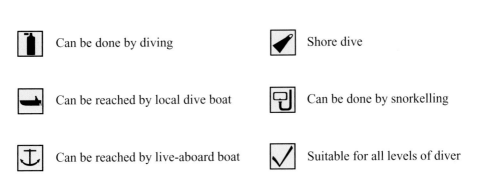

	Can be done by diving		Shore dive
	Can be reached by local dive boat		Can be done by snorkelling
	Can be reached by live-aboard boat		Suitable for all levels of diver

THE REGIONAL DIRECTORIES

A regional directory, which will help you plan and make the most of your trip, is included at the end of each regional section. Here you will find, where relevant, practical information on how to get to an area, where to stay and eat, and available dive facilities. Local non-diving highlights are also described, with suggestions for excursions.

OTHER FEATURES

At the start of the book you will find practical details and tips about travelling to and in the area, as well as a general introduction to Malta, Comino and Gozo. Also provided is a wealth of information about the general principles and conditions of diving in the area. Throughout the book there are features and small fact panels on topics of interest to divers and snorkellers. At the end of the book are sections on the marine environment (including coverage of marine life, conservation and codes of practice) and underwater photography and video. Also to be found here is information on health, safety and first aid, and a guide to marine creatures to look out for when diving in the Maltese islands.

INTRODUCTION TO MALTA, COMINO AND GOZO

A series of rugged islands set against the sparkling blue Mediterranean Sea, the Maltese archipelago lies 93km (58 miles) south of Sicily and 288km (180 miles) from the North African coast. Though frequently referred to simply as Malta, the Republic of Malta actually comprises three inhabited islands (Malta, Comino and Gozo) and a number of smaller, uninhabited islands, notably Cominotto, Filfla and St Paul's.

The island of Malta is the largest landmass, covering 246 sq km (95 sq miles), with a coastline of 136km (86 miles). Gozo is just over a quarter of this size, and barren-looking Comino – a designated nature reserve – is tiny by comparison. The archipelago consists for the most part of a limestone plateau with an ironstone shoreline and a series of low hills. For centuries farmers cultivated the arid land by creating terraces marked by drystone walls, many of which still criss-cross the islands today. Gozo is the most fertile of the islands, thanks to a rainwater-retaining layer of blue clay, and remains responsible for supplying much of the country's fruit and vegetables.

Thanks to their strategic position, located almost at the centre of the Mediterranean, the islands have attracted settlers and invaders throughout the centuries, who in turn have left an abundance of historic sites for visitors to explore. Monumental remains believed to predate the Pyramids, baroque churches and cathedrals, and imposing towers and fortresses all feature among the many topside attractions.

The magnificent capital, Valletta, overlooks an impressive network of harbours and creeks in the north of Malta. Across this island lies the pristine medieval city of Mdina, rising dramatically above the Maltese landscape. Gozo is dominated by its own citadel at Victoria, and Comino is best known for the Blue Lagoon, a haven for boat-trippers from the main islands. In all parts festivals are a frequent event, regularly showering brilliant fireworks across the night sky, while a variety of local crafts are still practised on Gozo and Malta, notably lacemaking.

Opposite: *Local fishing boats, or luzzu, are amongst the many craft in Kalkara boatyard near Valletta.*
Above: *A Gozitan farmer makes use of an improvised engine to power along his small cart.*

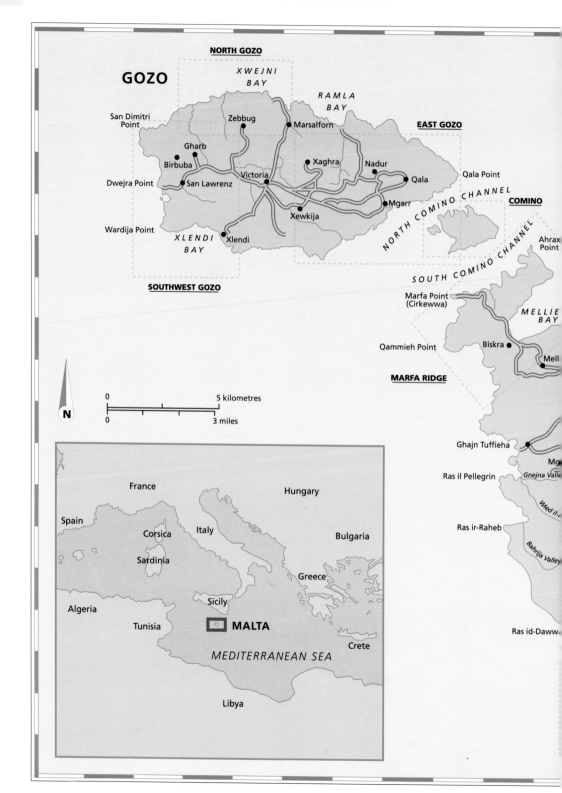

GOZO

NORTH GOZO

XWEJNI BAY

RAMLA BAY

EAST GOZO

San Dimitri Point

Zebbug

Marsalforn

Gharb

Birbuba

Xaghra

Nadur

Qala

Qala Point

COMINO

Dwejra Point

San Lawrenz

Victoria

Mgarr

Ahrax Point

Wardija Point

XLENDI BAY

Xlendi

Xewkija

NORTH COMINO CHANNEL

SOUTH COMINO CHANNEL

SOUTHWEST GOZO

Marfa Point (Cirkewwa)

MELLIE BAY

Qammieh Point

Biskra

Mell

MARFA RIDGE

N

0   5 kilometres

0   3 miles

Ghajn Tuffieha

Mg

Ras il Pellegrin

Gnejna Valle

France

Hungary

Wied il-

Spain

Corsica

Italy

Ras ir-Raheb

Bahrija Valley

Sardinia

Bulgaria

Algeria

Greece

Sicily

Tunisia

▫ **MALTA**

Crete

Ras id-Daww

MEDITERRANEAN SEA

Libya

MALTA, COMINO AND GOZO

MEDITERRANEAN SEA

MALTA

NORTH MALTA

ST PAUL'S BAY Qawra Point

Qrejten Point

Bahar ic-Caghag

Dragonara Point

Bugibba

Bur Marrad

St Julian's

VALLETTA AREA

Wied il-Faham

Wied il Ghasel

Wied Ghomor

Sliema

Naxxar

Ghajn Rihana Valley

St Elmo Point

Zebbiegh

Mosta

Msida

VALLETTA ■

GRAND HARBOUR

Ras il-Gebel

Birkirkara

Vittoriosa

Qlejgha Valley

Ta'l Isperanza Valley

Hamrun

Zabbar

Zonqor Point

Chadwick Lakes

Wied is-Sweda

Marsascala

Il-Gzira

Mtarfa

Wied il-Hemsija

Qormi

Fgura

Ghammieri

Zejtun

Il-Munxar

Mdina (Rabat)

Zebbug

Wied Qirda

Luqa

Ghaxaq

Wied Liemu

Wied Ta 'l-Isqof

Wied Baqqija

Wied Hanzit

Wied Dalam

Marsaxlokk

Siggiewi

Wied Has Sabtan

MARSAXLOKK BAY

Wied il-Luq

Birzebbuga

Delimara Point

Dingli

Girgenti Valley

Wied Xkora

Wied il-Qoton

Tal-Bajjada

Qrendi

Zurrieq

Kalafrana

Il-Kullana

Benghajsa Point

Ras Hamrija

Il-Minkba

SOUTH MALTA

THE MALTESE KNIGHTS

The Knights of the Order of St John were a powerful chivalric order, with a long history. First formed as a group of monks in Jerusalem, the order gradually extended its activities to escorting Christian pilgrims en route to Jerusalem, and then became a full military order. In 1530, after being expelled from their base in Rhodes by the Turkish fleet, the Knights were offered the use of Malta by Charles V. The order based itself at Birgu, building Fort St Angelo at the entrance to Dockyard Creek, where they stored their oar-driven galleys. Following the Great Siege, the Knights moved across the Grand Harbour to construct the fortified city of Valletta.

HISTORY

Separated from continental Europe and Africa some 10,000–12,000 years ago, the islands were first settled by Neolithic peoples arriving from Sicily in around 5000BC. These early inhabitants constructed magnificent temples such as the Ggantija temples on Gozo, built around 3600–3200BC, and the impressive Tarxien temples on Malta.

Phoenician traders arrived in the 9th century BC, using the islands as a staging post on their extensive maritime trading routes throughout the western Mediterranean and the Atlantic. They established settlements on the Grand Harbour and at Birgu (present-day Vittoriosa), and christened the islands *Maletha*, 'a place of shelter' or 'haven', from which the name Malta is derived. As Phoenician influence diminished, the islands' strategically advantageous position was contested by the Romans and a powerful Carthaginian empire to the south. Carthage was ousted in 218BC at the end of the second Punic War, and under subsequent Roman administration the islands enjoyed peace and prosperity for the next six centuries, becoming famous for exports of honey and cloth. In AD60 St Paul was shipwrecked here en route to trial in Rome and converted many islanders to Christianity.

With the collapse of Rome in the 4th century AD, Malta fell under the control of the Byzantine empire. Although relatively unaffected by the Islamic tide which swept westwards across North Africa in the 7th century, the islands were taken over by the Arabs in 870. Many Maltese converted to Islam and elements of Arabic were absorbed into the language, which has roots in Phoenician and Latin. Arab rule came to an end, however, in 1090 when the islands were annexed to Sicily by Count Roger the Norman, bringing back Christianity. Thereafter control of the islands passed through a succession of foreign nobles to Aragon (Spain). Stability was only achieved when in 1530 Charles V, Holy Roman Emperor and

Below: *The Ggantija temples on Gozo were built around 3600BC.*
Opposite: *Colourful pageantry takes place in the Citadel at Victoria, the capital of Gozo.*

King of Sicily and Spain, granted a home on Malta to the Knights of the Order of St John.

In May 1565 a massive Turkish campaign fleet of 181 ships and 35,000 men laid siege to the islands, which the Turks saw as a threat to their quest for territorial gains in southern Europe. The target of the first assault was Fort St Elmo, which succumbed after a month's continuous bombardment, though not without disastrous loss of life on both sides. The Turks then assailed forts St Angelo and St Michael for months, in what became known as the Great Siege, until a relief force finally arrived from Sicily and the Turks were routed.

After the Great Siege the Knights of St John built churches and defences as a sign of Malta's growing prosperity, but by the mid-18th century the Knights had fallen into disrepute and in 1798 Malta collapsed to Napoleon with scarcely a shot fired. The French in turn capitulated to the British in 1800, and British control of the islands was ratified by the Treaty of Paris in 1814. During World War I (1914–18) Malta became an 'island hospital', providing 25,000 beds for soldiers injured in the Dardanelles.

THE GEORGE CROSS

'To Honour her brave People I award the George Cross to the Island Fortress of Malta to bear witness to a Heroism and a Devotion that will long be famous in History.' King George VI

In April 1942, after 157 days of continuous aerial bombardment (compared to London's 57 days during the Blitz), Maltese morale was at its lowest point. In January and February alone, Malta had witnessed 499 air raid alerts, while for six weeks in March and April, some 6700 tons of bombs were dropped. In recognition of the islanders' heroic fortitude, King George VI bestowed the George Cross on Malta.

At the outbreak of World War II (1939–45) Malta formed Britain's most important naval base, protecting supply lines across the Mediterranean. Its importance became clear when the Germans launched their first air attack on the dockyards on 11 June 1940. Malta had few anti-aircraft defences and the islanders suffered innumerable hardships during the war, including severe rationing and almost continuous bombing.

Afterwards the British government donated £30 million to compensate for war damage and to help rebuild the economy. A new constitution was introduced in 1947, and the elections of 1962 saw the emergence of two principal parties, the Malta Labour Party and the Nationalist Party, both placing independence at the top of their manifesto. On 21 September 1964 Malta gained independence, with British ties being finally severed in 1979 when British forces withdrew. Malta finally became a member of the European Union in 2004.

Shipping plays an important part in the economy today, with Malta's dockyards successfully tendering for service and repair work on tankers and container ships plying the Mediterranean. However, tourism is now Malta's main industry, providing 36 per cent of the gross national income. Of the islands' one million annual visitors, 39 per cent are from Britain, with the next largest group, at 17 per cent, coming from Germany.

THE PEOPLE AND CULTURE

The Maltese are traditionally a hardworking and resilient people, pleased to welcome today's peaceable visitors – tourists, divers and sunseekers – from all over the world. While life on Malta is often carried out at a fast pace, affairs on Gozo tend to be more relaxed. Gozitans retain a separate identity – referring to their island by its 9th-century name, 'Ghawdex' – and only consider themselves secondly Maltese. All the islanders, Maltese and Gozitan alike, make good use of their leisure time and enjoy going to the beach at weekends.

Attitudes to dress are conventional, and Malta is a country of firm social traditions. The Maltese are devoted to family life; families are often large and usually stay closely in touch. Devoutly Roman Catholic, the islanders have over 357 churches, which can be seen everywhere, particularly in Gozo, where they dominate the skyline. Buildings generally have few windows, while inside marble floors and thick stonework help protect against the heat. Most are constructed from globigerina limestone, quarried on the islands, which characteristically displays varying shades of magnolia. Many of the older homes, and some new ones, have beautifully carved stonework balconies, a source of considerable family pride.

MALTESE TOURIST OFFICES

China
Malta Tourism Authority, 1-52, San Li Tun Diplomatic Office Bldg, Beijing 100600; tel/fax (0086) 10 65326716; e-mail: mtamlemb@public2.bta.net.cn.

France
Office du Tourisme de Malte, 9 Cité de Trevise 75009, Paris; tel (1) 48 00 03 79/fax (1) 48 00 04 41; e-mail: info@visitmalta.com.

Germany
Fremdenverkehrsamt Malta, Schillerstrasse 30–40, Frankfurt-am-Main, D-60313; tel (69) 285890/fax (69) 285479; e-mail: info@urlaubmalta.com.

Italy
Ente Nazionale per il Turismo di Malta, Via Gonzaga 7, 20123 Milan; tel (2) 867376, (2) 867395/fax (2) 874687; e-mail: info@malta.it.

The Netherlands
National Verkeersbureau Malta, Geelvinck Gebouw 4e, Singel 540, 1017 AZ Amsterdam; tel (20) 6207223/fax (20) 6207233; e-mail: info@malta.nl.

United Kingdom
Malta Tourist Office, Unit C, Park House, 14 Northfields, London. SW18 1DD; tel (020) 8877 6990/fax (020) 8874 9416; e-mail: uk@visitmalta.com.

USA and Canada
Malta Tourist Office, 65 Broadway, Suite 823, New York. NY10006; tel (212) 430 3779/fax (425) 795 3425; e-mail: office.us@visitmalta.com.

Russia
Embassy of Malta, Office 178, Bldg 1, ent 6,7, Korovy Val Street, Moscow 119049; tel (007) 095 0283819/fax (007) 095 2326413; e-mail: info@malta.ru.

LANGUAGE

Malti is the first language of the Maltese islands, originating from a Semitic language spoken by the Phoenicians and evolving over 2000 years through Arabic and European rule, with Greek, Italian, French and Spanish influences. English is widely used, and French, German and Italian may also be spoken. Street names are usually displayed bilingually.

A few basic words and expressions are listed. Any attempt to speak the language – however faltering – is much appreciated by the Maltese. Note that, throughout this book, local Malti names for marine life are given in square brackets.

BASIC WORDS	
Good morning	Bongu (*BON-joo*)
Good evening	Bonswa (*BON-swah*)
Goodbye	Sahha (*sah-har*)
Yes	Iva (*EE-vah*)
No	Le (*leh*)
Please	Jek joghgbok (*yehek YOJ-bok*)
Thank you	Grazzi (*GRAHT-see*)
Excuse me	Skuzi (*SKOO-zee*)
Cheers! (as in drinking)	Aviva! (*aviva*)

CLIMATE

Malta has an enviable climate. The islands are situated further south than some parts of the North African coast, and you can expect high temperatures, sometimes exceeding 30°C (90°F). From May/June through to the end of September maximum temperatures range from 29.5°C (85°F) to 33°C (92°F). Sun protection is strongly advised during the summer months.

From October through to March temperatures range between 17.2°C (64°F) and 27.9°C (82°F). The coolest time of the year is in the spring (March/April), with minimum temperatures around 9–11°C (48–52°F) and a maximum of 20–22°C (68–72°F).

The sun's strength is often disguised by sea breezes, particularly the northwesterly winds known as the *Majjistral*, at their strongest later in the year. The hot, dry *Sirocco* blows across from the Sahara in May and September, making the sea rough on the southern shores (during this time, all diving takes place on the northern shores). From late summer on, the *Grigal* blows from the northeast, and the northerly *Tramuntana* is sometimes responsible for winter storms.

From June to August, areas of high pressure lie over the islands and rainfall is almost non-existent. The first rains are in October or November, with December usually the wettest month.

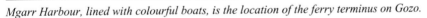

Mgarr Harbour, lined with colourful boats, is the location of the ferry terminus on Gozo.

TRAVELLING TO AND IN THE MALTESE ISLANDS

The Maltese archipelago receives over one million tourists each year, the majority arriving by air into the international airport 10km (6 miles) southwest of the islands' capital, Valletta. Over 85 per cent of visitors are from Europe, with flying time from major European airports such as London, Rome and Frankfurt being approximately 3 hours. **Air Malta** is the nation's principal carrier, while Lufthansa, Swissair, Alitalia, British Airways, Aeroflot, Balkan Airways, Transavia, Emirates and Tuninter all have regular connections into Malta. Air Malta's head office is at 285 Republic Street, Valletta, tel (356) 21690890; sales at Malta International Airport, tel (356) 21249600; www.airmalta.com.

Gozo can be reached by either helicopter or ferry connection from Malta. The heliport on Gozo is quite close to the ferry terminal at Mgarr, though most people travel to Gozo on the ferry from Cirkewwa.

Sea travellers to Malta can catch a ferry with the Italian line **Maresi Shipping** from Reggio di Calabria in Italy and from Catania in Sicily. There is also a high-speed catamaran service from Pozzalo in Sicily operated by **Virtu Ferries**. Lastly, **Sea Malta** operates a ferry from Tripoli on a daily basis.

VISAS AND PERMITS

UK and other European nationals can travel to Malta on a full passport. Most countries' nationals are permitted entry without a visa, but bear in mind that regulations may change. Always ask your travel agent to check before booking your trip. Nationals of countries that do require a visa should obtain these from their nearest Maltese embassy or consulate, or should apply in writing to the Police Headquarters, Floriana, Malta, VLT15; tel (356) 21224001/fax (356) 21247777 and 21235308. If you plan to stay for longer than three months, you must apply in person to the Principal Immigration Officer at the Police Headquarters well before the end of your initial three-month stay.

Opposite: *The Blue Lagoon on Comino is probably the most popular tourist attraction in the islands.*
Above: *Many local fishing boats, or luzzu, are brilliantly coloured.*

FLOATING TAXIS

One traditional form of transport is the *dghajsa* (pronounced 'dyesa'), Malta's answer to the gondola. These high-prowed and brightly painted water taxis ply across the Grand Harbour, and were once used to ferry British sailors back to their ships. Originally propelled by a standing oarsman, they now rely on outboard motors and are mainly found along Senglea's waterfront. If you visit the Grand Harbour on 8 September you will be able to see the colourful annual *dghajsa* races.

CUSTOMS AND IMMIGRATION

Immigration forms must be filled in prior to passing through passport control in Malta; forms are usually handed out on aeroplanes in advance. Customs officers are well used to the thousands of divers who arrive in Malta laden with baggage, and they generally let you walk straight through after a cursory examination of your documents and questions about your diving destination. However, you may be asked if you are carrying a speargun, since speargun fishing is illegal. Note that, if you are carrying lots of photographic equipment, it is advisable to write a list of contents, any serial numbers and the value of each item. This list can be presented to customs and stamped on arrival, and should later be checked and cleared on departure.

TRANSPORT

Taxis are available at the airport and ferry terminals and around the main hotels. All taxis are white, clearly marked 'TAXI' and have white number plates. They all have meters and drivers can give you an estimate of the cost in advance of your trip if asked. Note that there is a fixed scale of fares from the airport, payable on a ticketing basis; tickets are available at a kiosk in the airport. Taxi fares from hotels to the airport work on a different scale of charges and journeys of this kind will be more expensive. A small tip of around 10 per cent is expected if the driver has been helpful.

Hiring a taxi and driver for the day, between four people, and asking for an unofficial guided tour, can be a great way to see the area and is usually relatively inexpensive.

The local **bus** service is extensive and routes cover both the main islands. The central bus terminal on Malta is opposite the Triton Fountain outside the City Gate in Valletta. The terminal on Gozo is on Main Gate Street in Victoria (Rabat). Routes are indicated by numbers, which are displayed on notice boards at bus stations. Bus maps are also freely available.

Car hire is an obvious alternative, particularly when travelling on Gozo. You need a valid driver's licence from your country of origin and to purchase and carry proof of car insurance. Rental agencies always require a signed credit card imprint as a deposit, and without a credit card you will not be able to hire a car. Generally, rental prices are very competitive.

Collect your hire car, jeep or moped early in the day to ensure you have the pick of the better models. Check the vehicle prior to rental to avoid any unnecessary problems later on and pay particular attention to the tyres, including the spare in the boot. Maltese roads are notoriously bad and tyres on many rental cars are worn; punctures are commonplace. Should you experience a puncture, a repair will cost from Lm 2.5.

Driving is on the left, overtaking on the right. All distance markers are in kilometres. Be sure to keep the car filled as fuel stations are few and far between, and most are closed on Sunday – though a number have 'automatic' pumps which can be used until 22:00 during the week and between 08:00 and noon on Sunday. Note that parking in the walled city of Valletta

---

PUBLIC HOLIDAYS

Public holidays observed in Malta are:

1 January	New Year's Day
10 February	St Paul's Shipwreck
19 March	St Joseph's Day
Variable	Good Friday
31 March	Freedom Day
1 May	Labour Day
7 June	Commemoration of 7 June 1919
29 June	Feast of St Peter and St Paul (*Mnarja*)
15 August	Assumption (*Santa Marija*)
8 September	Our Lady of Victories
21 September	Independence Day
8 December	Feast of the Immaculate Conception
13 December	Republic Day
25 December	Christmas Day

Little traffic permeates Mdina's quiet streets other than these traditional karrozini.

can be very difficult, so it is best to park outside the city and travel in by taxi or water taxi or on foot. Air Malta have a special deal with Europcar for car rental at favourable rates.

MONEY
The Malta Lira (Lm) is divided into 100 cents (c). Coins come in denominations of 1c, 2c, 5c, 10c, 25c, 50c and Lm 1, and notes in Lm 2, Lm 5, Lm 10 and Lm 20.

Cash, **travellers' cheques** and **Eurocheques** can be exchanged at banks, most hotels and restaurants, and larger shops. Although banks are usually the best place to change money, the airport also offers competitive exchange rates. There is no restriction on the amount of foreign currency that can be imported by individual visitors to Malta, although the amount of Maltese money carried into Malta is restricted to Lm 50 per person. All of the major **credit cards** are accepted by most hotels, restaurants and a large number of retail outlets. Now that Malta is part of the European Union, the Euro is widely accepted in hotels and larger shops and restaurants; however the change may well be in Maltese Pounds and the exchange rate can be diabolical! The exchange rate for US Dollars is even worse.

ELECTRICITY
The electrical supply in Malta is 240 volts, single phase, 50 cycles; 13 amp, British-style three-pin rectangular sockets are used. Visitors will need to bring an adaptor for any appliances such as a 110 volt recharger for lamps or electronic equipment. Most hotels have dual 220/110 shaver sockets and hair dryers.

CAR BREAKDOWN AGENCIES
There are three reputable breakdown agencies offering a 24hr service:
CAA
Malta: tel (356) 21696696/fax (356) 21696969
MTC
Malta: tel (356) 21333332
RMF
Malta: tel (356) 21242222/fax (356) 21246354; Gozo: tel 21558844

FILM MAKING IN MALTA

Malta has gradually come to the forefront of filmmaking after Robert Altman directed *Popeye* in 1979. The film location, Popeye Village, is at Anchor Bay on Malta and is still a huge tourist attraction. To reach it, take bus 44 or 45 from Valletta bus terminus to Mellieha Bay, continuing on foot for 1km (¹/₂ mile) west to Anchor Bay.

Latterly, Gozo was used as the setting for some scenes of *The League of Extraordinary Gentlemen*; Comino was used for *The Count of Monte Christo*; the massive sea tank to the south of Malta was used for *Waterworld* with Kevin Costner and *Master and Commander* with Russell Crowe. The island has also been used recently as the set for two Hollywood blockbusters: *Troy* and *Alexander*.

BUSINESS HOURS AND SHOPPING

In common with other Mediterranean countries, Malta observes the *siesta*, a three-hour break after lunch, which for most people is usually a family affair taken at home. Almost all shops open at 08:00 and close for *siesta* between noon and 13:00, reopening at 16:00 until 19:00. Some village shops open even earlier, from 07:00, to cater to schoolchildren. Gift shops tend to stay open from 09:00 until 19:00, while pharmacies often operate longer hours, 08:00–12:30 and 15:30–19:00. Pharmacists can dispense medication for minor complaints, but if the problem is more serious, seek medical advice.

Apart from a Marks & Spencer and a British Home Stores in both Valletta and Sliema, Malta has very few large stores, and most general shopping is done at small family-run shops or in the marketplace. Haggling is not an accepted practice, although you may be able to negotiate with individual street vendors. Vendors can usually be found at the roadside by popular beaches selling a variety

Mellieha Bay in the northeast of Malta is a well established destination for holidaymakers.

of fruit, snacks and drinks. Quality, locally made lace can be purchased in a number of shops, but make sure it is genuinely hand-made.

PERSONAL SAFETY

There is very little crime in Malta and personal possessions will be more than secure within hotel safes or safety deposit boxes. There are no beggars and pedlars will not accost you on beaches. Police stations (mostly marked by a blue light outside) are manned round the clock. Visitors from the UK will recognize the uniform, almost identical to that worn by the British police. You should report any crime to the police immediately, and, in the case of a car accident, leave your vehicle where it is. If you have your camera with you, take a photograph of the cars *in situ*.

CLOTHING

Swimwear is strictly for the beach or swimming pool terraces and it is unacceptable for women to wear bikini tops when shopping downtown, for example. Visitors should avoid wearing tight or flashy clothes, as they can invite the wrong sort of attention. The official line is that topless sunbathing is banned throughout Malta, though in reality this is not always the case. In any event, have respect for local sensibilities.

SPORTS

The Maltese islands offer several sporting opportunities for non-divers, including a **golf** course on the main island of Malta, between Valletta and the international airport. For details contact **The Marsa Sports and Country Club**, Triq Aldo Moro, Marsa, tel (356) 21233851, or **The Royal Malta Golf Club**, Triq Aldo Moro, Marsa, tel (356) 21230664. There are no golf courses on Gozo as yet, but one is being planned at the Ta' Cenc Hotel. **Tennis** is very popular for those wanting to keep fit between dives. All of the large international resort hotels have their own tennis courts or access to courts nearby. The Comino Hotel is particularly popular with tennis lovers.

Fishing is something of a national pastime in the Maltese archipelago, with shallow reefs around the shores teeming with small fish. All the major international resort hotels have **windsurfing** boards for hire and a large number also offer instruction, often at little or no additional cost. Many of the bays on all three islands are relatively exposed, so there is usually somewhere with wind. Mellieha Bay is considered excellent for windsurfing, with above-average facilities available from Aquaventure.

PRACTICAL DOS AND DON'TS

- **Suntanning:** The most common health problems experienced by visitors come from underestimating the power of the sun, especially when there is a light breeze, so avoid direct sunlight between 10:00 and 14:00. The use of protective sun cream is recommended, especially for fair-skinned people (a minimum of factor 25). Particular attention should be paid to the top of the head (by wearing a hat), the nose, backs of the knees and tops of the feet.
- **Food:** In the summer months food does not last long out of a refrigerator. Make sure that all food is freshly cooked and eat it while still hot. Avoid cooked food that is not stored in a cold cabinet.
- **Water:** Tap water is safe to drink throughout the islands, with over 60 per cent processed using reverse osmosis, which leaves a slightly unpleasant taste as it is desalinated seawater. Local and imported bottled water is readily available and sold in restaurants and bars, although it is much cheaper in local shops and supermarkets. Bottled water does vary in price and local 'tourist' shops will certainly overcharge and some may even discriminate between locals and tourists!
- **Insects:** Insect bites are annoying and can cause an allergic reaction in some people, so it is best to use an insect repellent, especially at dusk and dawn. While diving at night, be prepared for mosquitoes; they can be huge.
- **Personal Safety:** Never leave any valuables or scuba diving equipment on show in a car, particularly if parked in a secluded area. If there is a theft, always remember to obtain a crime report number for your travel insurance claim.

EMERGENCY NUMBERS

General Hospital (Malta)	tel (356) 21241251
General Hospital (Gozo)	tel (356) 21 561600
Hyperbaric Unit (Malta)	tel (356) 21234766, (356) 21259549
Emergency	tel 112
Ambulance	tel 196
Fire	tel 199
Police	tel 191
Air rescue	tel (356) 21244371
Sea rescue	tel (356) 21238797

DIVING AND SNORKELLING IN THE MALTESE ISLANDS

The Maltese islands are one of the top diving destinations in the Mediterranean, popular with German, Italian, Dutch, Scandinavian and British divers. The annual number of visiting divers currently amounts to around 50,000, who undertake an average of ten dives each, giving a staggering total of 500,000 dives around the islands each year. The offer of unlimited diving, clear deep water and an unrivalled abundance of marine life keeps divers coming back.

Malta was the top overseas destination for British divers before the Red Sea opened to mass tourism, and more recently the islands have been enjoying a resurgence in popularity. There is growing local concern to protect marine life, new conservation policies have been set out, and the Maltese are keen to develop a sustainable future for marine tourism.

Malta, Comino and Gozo once formed an ancient land link with the island of Sicily some 93km (58 miles) to the north. The waters which wash around the narrow constrictions between the islands are rich in nutrients, providing ideal conditions for marine flora and fauna to flourish. Huge schools of salema (*Sarpa salpa*) can be found feeding on algae off Crocodile Rock at Dwejra Point (Gozo, Site 14), while shoals of sand smelt, bogue and bream typically cluster around the wreck of the *Rozi* at Cirkewwa (Malta, Site 26).

All three islands are rich in diving opportunities. Much of the best diving is done on Gozo, with day-trip cars and dive-centre vehicles making the ferry crossing from Malta several times daily. Comino also has some interesting dive sites. A surprise for many visitors is the exceptionally scenic quality of the diving around the archipelago. In addition to reef structures offshore, there is exciting and challenging cave diving in the spectacular caverns, chimneys and gullies for which these islands are famed.

Much of the diving can be done from the shore and, once you have found your way around, it is possible to make any number of unescorted dives virtually anywhere. However, extreme care should be taken, as the rocky foreshore is extremely sharp and jagged; it is recommended that all divers and snorkellers wear protective shoes or hard-soled booties for entry to and exit

Opposite: *Marfa Point at the western end of Malta is perfect for shore diving in safe waters.*
Above: *The inquisitive Turkish wrasse (Thalassoma pavo) is found in shallow coastal waters.*

from a shore dive. A great deal of the diving around the islands is done independently, with many coming to the island to dive on their own. In such circumstances it is important to do your own pre-dive planning and stick to it. If you are diving from a shore location, whether by day or by night, inform your hotel or someone reliable of your dive plan and the approximate time of your exit from the water.

If you are diving with one of the local dive shops, dive masters will plan your dive and dive time. Unless you are part of a class learning to dive, a typical day's diving consists of a morning deep dive to approximately 36m (120ft). The second dive of the day will usually be in the afternoon and may be another deep dive, although it is more often a much shallower dive somewhere else around the coastline. Night diving is a further possibility and there are a number of suitable shore diving locations fairly close to the hotel centres, such as the Dwejra Blue Hole, Marfa Point and Mgarr Ix-Xini.

There are literally hundreds of recorded dive sites around the Maltese islands' coastline, as well as many offshore reefs and shoals. Sites may be known by either local Malti names or names given by the dive centres who favour them. This quite often leads to misunderstanding, since some are part of the same reef; we have tried to clarify these where feasible.

Mediterranean Reefs

While the term 'reef' is used throughout this book, it is important to note that there are no true coral reefs in the Mediterranean. Tropical coral reefs are formed over thousands of years by living organisms which build over the skeletons of their ancestors, always expanding upwards towards the light. The seabed in Malta consists rather of an ancient limestone and sandstone rock base which was thrust upwards by volcanic upheaval many centuries ago and further shaped by the raising and lowering of the oceans during various ice ages. The submarine ridges and boulder slopes are referred to as reefs principally because they are separate from the shoreline. Many are nonetheless completely encrusted by small colonizing cup corals, bryozoans, algae and hydroids.

Diving Conditions

The majority of the diving around Malta, Comino and Gozo is from the shore and these dives are always treated as potential deep dives. The strongest currents are located off the extremities of each island, but they very rarely pose any threat to divers. If you are unsure of your ability in strong current, always check with the dive master on the boat from which you are diving.

By far the greatest danger is the accessibility of potentially very hazardous deep cavern and penetration dives to even the most inexperienced diver. Deep diving is so easy around the islands that all too many unescorted tourists risk repetitive dives to over 60m (200ft), and this has resulted in a number of fatalities. Although these deaths are linked to a variety of factors (inexperience, lack of proper equipment, diving in adverse weather conditions), the problem is usually one of inexperienced divers going too deep in crystal clear water and discovering that they have run out of air too quickly in a cavern at depth.

Surge conditions can be a problem when diving close to shore, and preferred entry and exit points are sheltered locations where divers can get in and out of the water safely, such as Dwejra Point and Marfa Point. During the periodic autumn storms which the islands experience, diving in the harbour at Valletta really comes into its own. Here you can

---

Diving Conditions and Seabed Structures

Diving conditions vary little around the coastline and visiting divers will experience reef conditions comparable to those found elsewhere in the central Mediterranean. The reef structures are:

Pinnacle: a large, ancient coralline limestone head, tower-shaped.

Boulder: huge blocks of tumbled-down limestone which form irregular reefs all around the coastline.

Canyon: a vertical cut in the coastal headland.

Tunnel: a hole running through the reef, also sometimes known as a swimthrough, ravine or crevice.

Chimney: generally a narrow tunnel running vertically up through the edge of the reef.

Shelf: where the deep water begins.

Wall or Cliff: the land cliff that forms the shelf by plunging underwater.

explore shipwrecks from World War II in fairly calm conditions and, although the water visibility is comparatively low, these are still worthwhile dives. The Italian Mission and the National Tourism Organization have begun to improve the shore access to many other dive sites and are generally making entry and exit points much safer, for example by installing hand rails and new steps.

VISIBILITY

Underwater visibility is usually excellent and rarely influenced by tide and current, although it does depend on location and the time of year. Visibility alters during the long oceanic swell which sometimes piles in waves across the Mediterranean and virtually puts paid to any diving along the east coasts of Malta and Gozo when it occurs (though there are sheltered alternative sites at such times like Dwejra Point, Xlendi Bay and Cirkewwa). Visibility may be reduced when shallow, sandy lagoons are stirred up or, as in all island and coastal locations, as a result of the seasonal influxes of plankton which cloud the water in spring and autumn. After heavy rainfall, the islands' inshore valleys such as Xlendi Bay and the Ghasri Valley can have visibility reduced to nil; fortunately these are particularly tidal areas next to deep water and the sediment soon washes out over the edge of the continental shelf. In general terms, of course, the further you are from any major rainwater run-off, the better the visibility.

During the summer visibility hardly ever exceeds 25m (80ft), but it can soar staggeringly in the winter between November and March to as much as 45m (150ft). The shallow bays and Valletta harbour are perhaps the least impressive, with an average visibility of around 6m (20ft) in the summer and 12m (40ft) in winter.

In late summer Cassiopeia jellyfish (Cothyloriza tubercolata) are common around the islands.

MALTA'S BEST BEACHES

Most of Malta's 11 sandy beaches are situated in the north of the island. The most popular are Mellieha Bay, Golden Sands, Ghajn Tuffieha Bay and Gneja Bay on Malta, and Ramla Bay and San Blas Bay on Gozo. There are also two sandy beaches on Comino. The Maltese love the sea and are rarely to be found near swimming pools or fresh water, known locally as 'sweet water'. They particularly enjoy meeting friends and family on the beach at weekends or public holidays.

An extensive programme exists to monitor the quality of the bathing water, in compliance with EU 'Blue Flag' policies. Samples are analysed by the Department of Health in conjunction with the Environment Protection Department and detailed reports are published every year. The beaches and foreshore are cleaned by a special section within the Tourism Secretariat.

Dive Boats

Although most diving is from the shore, there are shallow reef dives offshore and some superb walls to the southeast of both Malta and Gozo, as well as the best dives on Comino, which are accessible only by boat. There are two kinds of dive boat. The slower kind are converted local fishing boats, or *luzzu*, which are generally hired by dive resorts for day diving and which leave from Marfa. These carry enough air on board for two dives, with about an hour and a half's rest between dives. Such a trip usually leaves around 10:00 and is out for around 6 hours, so take a packed lunch. Then there are a number of much faster dedicated dive boats, such as the one used by St Andrew's Divers' Cove on Gozo. These can reach out-of-the-way locations such as San Dimitri Point relatively quickly.

Entry into the water from a *luzzu* is generally from the side of the craft, by means of a giant step forward. Entry from a dedicated dive boat may be either by a backwards roll or by slipping over the side while keeping one hand on the boat.

Private boat charter is readily available. One of the best inflatable-type boats is run by Simon Theuma of Diverse Sea (www.diverse-sea.com); he is well informed and equipped to visit deeper wrecks such as the Beaufighter, Bristol Blenheim, Le Polynesean, Stubborn, E Boat and the Hellespont.

Learning to Dive

There are over 40 diving operations registered with the Maltese Ministry of Tourism and several others (mainly German) that operate seasonally from various hotels. There are also a number of very professional diving companies who choose not to be registered with the Ministry of Tourism or the Diving Association. It is not our intention to make judgements, but we have only listed those diving schools and centres that have an operating licence. A full list is available from branches of the Maltese Tourist Office overseas (see page 16), or from the Federation of Underwater Activities in Malta (FUAM), PO Box 29, Gzira, Malta.

Many thousands of experienced scuba divers visit Malta, Comino and Gozo each year. Most are familiar with the area's dive sites and know the particular locations they want to revisit, only using the local dive shops to hire air bottles and air refills. Nevertheless, clear, warm water all year round also makes the Maltese islands a perfect location for learning to dive.

When choosing a dive operation, make sure it is affiliated to one of the major schools of instruction such as PADI, CMAS or BSAC. PADI (Professional Association of Diving Instructors) is probably the most popular training system in the archipelago, though most larger dive operators have instructors qualified with at least two or three different organizations. BSAC (British Sub Aqua Club) has instructors attached to a number of resorts, as does CMAS (Confédération Mondiale d'Activités Subaquatiques – World Underwater Federation), the other principal body for diving certification in Europe. Two other diving associations with a presence in Malta are FUAM (see above), which is affiliated to CMAS, and APDS (Association of Professional Diving Schools), which can be contacted through the Secretary, APDS, Msida Court, 6 1/2 Msida Sea Front, Msida, Malta.

If you only have a few days you can take a resort course. This is designed to give a taste of diving and fire your enthusiasm, as well as teaching basic water safety and conservation, with

Above: *A dive boat heads for the Blue Dome, at the mouth of the Ghasri Valley (Gozo, Site 7).*
Below: *Many walls teem with colourful invertebrates such as this starfish.*

2–4 hours of instruction. Resort courses are aimed at people aged 12 and over (under 18s must have full parental consent) with no upper age limit. The cost includes full rental equipment.

If you decide to take your training further you can go on the 5-day Open Water certification course (under the PADI system). This gives you the opportunity to dive on several of the islands' fabulous sites with a fully qualified dive instructor to a maximum depth of 18m (60ft).

On passing the Open Water course, divers are then able to enrol on an Advanced Open Water course. Thereafter it is possible to choose from a wide variety of speciality courses, such as wreck diving, underwater photography or training to be an instructor. One dive resort, Aquaventure at the Mellieha Bay Hotel on Malta, runs courses for cave and cavern diving.

Once you are fully qualified, your certification or 'C' card serves as your diving passport and is recognized worldwide. It is valid for life, though if you are unable to dive from one year to the next, it is recommended that you enrol on a refresher course.

MALTESE DIVING STANDARDS

Visitors who wish to dive independently no longer need a Maltese Diving Permit, but must register with a dive shop and pay a small fee towards the Malta Marine Foundation, which is a fund set aside to protect, preserve and develop dive sites around the islands. For qualified divers wishing to rent equipment, they must be at least of an Advanced Open Water standard and certainly BSAC Sports Diver, CMAS two-star diver or above. All you need to do is present your diving qualification to a diving centre and fill in the necessary forms. Any diver

Seen here from San Dimitri Point is the Divemania from St Andrew's Divers Cove.

below this grade can only dive with a Maltese registered instructor. Divers are not allowed into the water unaccompanied and must either have a 'buddy' or accompanying instructor. Now that the diving industry comes under the remit of the Tourism Office and not the Department of Health, diving medicals are no longer required for visiting Sports Divers. Self-declaration is sufficient, however if there are any contra-indications answered on the statement, a local medical will be required.

Any instructor wishing to take responsibility for divers must be issued with a temporary ID card for the duration of their holiday and must present a current medical certificate from an approved doctor in diving medicine. An Instructor's Medical can be obtained on Malta and Gozo and at present costs Lm 10. Instructors should also present a full list of approved and up-to-date qualifications as well as two approved, passport ID photographs.

Independent divers must have a float supporting a white and blue (code A) flag, which must be displayed on all dives. All diving equipment must be in good order and divers must not dive in restricted areas (which are indicated in all licensed dive shops) or take anything that may be of historical importance – anything of this nature should be reported to the Museum Department.

DEEP DIVING

More and more diving businesses are now geared up for deep diving in all of its forms. Most companies now offer NITROX as standard for extended, safer time at shallower depths. Trimix is now readily available and many locals and visitors dive with closed circuit or semi-closed circuit rebreathers. These able and qualified deep-water trained divers are responsible for the discovery and exploration of the numerous war casualties that litter the seabed around the islands. Deep diving courses are now available through many of the diving schools on both Malta and Gozo.

DISABLED DIVERS

A number of diving operations are equipped for instructing disabled divers, with boats specially adapted for wheelchairs, and docks and entry points allowing easy access. Dive centres are able to certify individuals with a range of disabilities, provided that they are medically able to dive. Any prospective student must see a physician prior to taking a certification course.

The general rule in the Maltese islands is that any dive operator with its own jetty will offer help for disabled divers. Many smaller dive operators are constrained because access to the dive boat is by walking down a rocky and sandy beach, followed by wading out to chest-deep water. However, services are continually being improved and up-to-date information can be obtained from the Federation of Underwater Activities in Malta (FUAM) or by contacting the Maltese Department of Tourism.

NITROGEN NARCOSIS

Many dives around the Maltese islands are deep dives, rendering the possibility of being affected by nitrogen narcosis comparatively high. Remember that narcosis is serious and not something to be played around with. If you are planning to dive deep, first take a deep diving course, then increase your depth gradually 3m (10ft) at a time. The symptoms of nitrogen narcosis (also known as the 'rapture of the deep') are akin to euphoria or drunkenness.

PREVENTION OF THE BENDS

Do: drink plenty of water (to prevent dehydration);

dive conservatively (don't push the tables or computer).

Don't: over-exercise before or after diving;

drink too much alcohol or coffee;

take hot showers after diving;

let your body get too cold during or after diving.

If a diver experiences minor tingling, numbness, extreme fatigue, weakness, dizziness, vertigo, or general health problems, take action by following the steps outlined on page 103. If necessary contact the **Hyperbaric Chamber**; tel (356) 21234766.

For further details on organizations and training, contact:

BSAC, Telfords Quay, Ellesmere Port, South Wirral, Cheshire L65 4FY, UK; tel (+44) (0)151 350 6200/fax (+44) (0)151 350 6215.

National Commission for the Handicapped, St Joseph's High Rd, Santa Venera, Malta; tel (356) 21487789.

SNORKEL TIPS, TECHNIQUES AND EQUIPMENT

Snorkelling is a sport for all ages and can be done on your own, with a partner or even as a family. There is absolutely no age limit on snorkelling and many hours of enjoyment can be had as long as you are in safe, protected waters.

Entering the water for the first time wearing a mask, snorkel and fins can be daunting, but with the correct techniques you will quickly discover that snorkelling requires little physical effort. Only the ability to swim is essential. Snorkelling is also a recommended way to get gentle exercise and can be both physically and mentally stimulating, though people with a medical condition should consult a doctor first.

With correct instruction you will quickly be able to enjoy sites suitable for snorkelling, such as the splendid Blue Lagoon on Comino or feeding the fish at the Santa Marija Caves. It is wise to check with the local dive shop whether the area you are planning to snorkel in is safe enough for you and your family. If in any doubt, do not enter the water, and seek advice first.

Instruction is offered at many local dive centres and hotels and may take place in a dive centre's swimming pool. Equipment can normally be rented from a dive shop, though snorkelling it not an expensive sport and it is possible to purchase your own.

SNORKELLING AND DIVING EQUIPMENT

Snorkelling equipment consists primarily of a snorkel and a mask with an adjustable strap and toughened glass. The mask must be of a kind that enables you to adjust the air pressure inside through your nose. Several types have the provision for optical lenses to be installed. For those who wear contact lenses, a close fitting, low volume mask should be adequate. The snorkel should not be too long or have too wide a bore, as you need to be able to clear the water out of it in a single breath if you submerge yourself too far. Some snorkels have a self-draining device which removes any excess water. The snorkel must fit snugly in the mouth and be free of any type of restriction that might impair breathing.

Fins, or flippers, are an important piece of equipment, available in two different styles. One has an adjustable ankle strap and is worn over diving boots. A smaller, softer kind can be worn on bare feet, fitting closely around the foot.

In addition to the basic equipment of mask, snorkel and fins, it is sensible to wear a Lycra swim-skin or a thin full wetsuit. This will not only shield you from the sun's rays, but also afford protection against any stinging microscopic plankton found in the water. If you have no other protection, at least wear a T-shirt to keep off the sun's rays.

SWIMMING SAFETY TIPS

- Use caution when swimming in unfamiliar areas.
- Take care not to swim when overtired, overheated or directly after eating.
- Children should be supervised in surf and when using inflatable objects.
- If caught in an undertow, do not panic. Rather than try to swim directly back to the shore, swim parallel to the shore for a few metres unti you find you are clear of the undertow – then swim to shore.
- Keep clear of the rocky shoreline.

BUOYANCY CONTROL

To protect marine life, divers must master the art of buoyancy control. The essential thing is to be able to hover both horizontally and vertically close to the reef or the bottom without needing to touch either. Buoyancy is controlled by inflating or deflating your buoyancy compensator at various depths. Once expert buoyancy is achieved, you will notice a drastic reduction in your air consumption; you will see more marine life on each dive; you will dramatically cut down on accidental environmental damage; and your pleasure will increase proportionately.

The impressive Blue Hole (Gozo, Site 12) invariably attracts large numbers of divers.

Supplementing the basic snorkelling equipment, diving equipment consists of an air tank and air; a regulator or demand valve through which you breathe; a contents gauge to indicate how much air you have left in your tank; an easy-to-read depth gauge to indicate your current depth and maximum depth reached; a watch with an adjustable bezel or timer device to let you know how long you have been at a specific depth and the duration of your dive; a weight belt and weights, which help counteract the body's natural buoyancy; and a buoyancy compensator or life jacket of some description that allows you to adjust buoyancy at depth in order to remain at depth or keep off the reef. As the water temperature around the Maltese islands drops to 14°C (57°F) during the winter months, it is also advisable to wear a full wetsuit or, better still, a drysuit for additional comfort.

A small knife may be worn, in case you need to use it to cut yourself free from impediments such as fishing line loose in the water. A computer is recommended for more experienced divers who are on an unlimited dive package, to assist them with repetitive dive profiles.

SNORKEL TIPS

- Clean your mask before snorkelling by wetting it first, then spitting into it and spreading the saliva with your fingers. Finally, rinse out the mask. This process prevents the mask from 'fogging'.
- When putting the mask on, make sure your hair does not become trapped under the seal of the mask.
- If water enters the mask, breathe out through your nose whilst holding the top of the mask firmly to the forehead.
- If water does enter the breathing tube, blow sharply through the tube to expel it.
- Always snorkel with a partner.

MALTA

M alta, the largest island of the archipelago, covers 246 sq km (95 sq miles), with a coastline of 136km (86 miles), and is characterized by high southern cliffs sloping gently to the heavily indented coast in the north. Some 90 per cent of the population lives in or around the Valletta area, comprising the fortified capital Valletta, the historical Three Cities (Vittoriosa, Cospicua and Senglea) and the modern resort of Sliema. Further tourist development exists along the northern coast at St Julian's and St Paul's Bay, while the centre of the island is dominated by the medieval walled city of Mdina.

The majority of the diving in Malta can be done from the shore. For the purpose of this book, we have divided the island into four areas. The **Valletta area**, including Marsamxett Harbour and the Grand Harbour, was the scene of massive aerial bombardment during World War II and now contains a large number of wrecks. Many of these are on major shipping routes and consequently are out of bounds. However, two wrecks – HMS *Maori* and the barge *Carolita* (sites 5 and 6) – are perfect for exploration, while other accessible wrecks are the Tent Peg Wreck, MV *Odile* and HMS *Jersey*.

Several sites can be found along the **north** of the island, as well as very deep wrecks like HMS *Stubborn* (see box, page 40), an intact submarine in 60m (200ft). Because these wrecks are regarded as too deep for sport divers on holiday, however, they are not described in full in this book.

More accessible is Cirkewwa (or Marfa Point, as it is more commonly known) on the popular **Marfa Ridge**, a magnet for dive training and for more experienced divers who want to dive the wreck of the *Rozi* (Site 26). The area around the ferry port has been fully redeveloped and all of the dive sites in the Cirkewwa zone are fully accessible to divers of all standards. However there are still no toilet facilities for divers near the dive sites and divers still suffer the problem of hassle from local fishermen.

Opposite: *Golden Bay takes its name from the colour of its sandy beach.*
Above: *The bearded fireworm (Hermodice carunculata) is common around the Maltese islands.*

In the **south** of the island, the caves and cliffs to the southeast are spectacular. As well as the relatively unexplored island of Filfla, there are also six new wreck sites along the southeast and south coasts. These are the Beaufighter at Sliema, the *Hellespont* and the E. Boat outside Valletta, the Blenheim Bomber near Marsaxlokk and *Le Polynesien* also in the vicinity. The *Um El Faroud* sunk in 1998, is now very popular in the south near the blue Grotto, although the wreck is now split in two and inevitably there will be severe deterioration in the coming years.

Generally the diving is scenic, with wonderful walls, spectacular natural archways, caves, caverns and wrecks contributing to the overall pleasure of the dive. Fish life is much more profuse than you may have been led to believe, with huge shoals of damselfish, bream, bogue and smelt to be encountered on most sites. Several areas are popular for fish feeding, and, although there are reservations about the possible effect this may have on natural ecological processes, many snorkelling and diving tourists come to enjoy the spectacle of being surrounded by thousands of fish.

Night diving is also very popular and most dive centres offer night diving several times a week. For the many visitors diving independently, of course, there is no limit to the number and type of dives you can undertake.

A word of caution. There are a vast number of submarine caves and caverns around the islands, many of which extend for hundreds of metres underground, as well as several spectacular natural arches. Remember that cave and cavern diving is a specialized activity and divers should not try to explore such sites without qualified guides or the proper training.

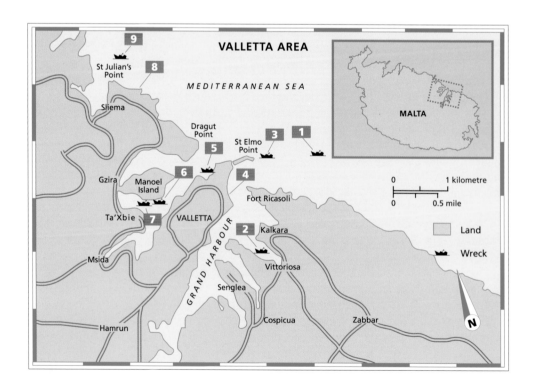

The Beaufighter 'N' is one of a number of ships and aircraft lost during World War II.

1 HELLESPONT
★★★

Location: Offshore to the northeast of St Elmo Point at Valletta.
Access: By boat only.
Conditions: Exposed site, so it can be choppy with some current.
Average depth: 35m (125ft)
Maximum depth: 40m (135ft)
Average visibility: 12m (40ft)

Built for HM Government by Earle's Shipbuilding and Engineering Company of Hull, the *Hellespont* was launched on 10 May 1910, and her dimensions were 44.2m (145ft) by 8.5m (28ft) with a draught of 3.75m (12ft). The *Hellespont* was a former paddle steamer that worked as a supply boat around the naval yards during World War I. On the night of 7 September 1940, she was bombed and damaged by an Italian aircraft and was mothballed. She was then bombed on 6 April 1942 and her bows were completely destroyed. After the war, the Maltese authorities decided to clear the harbours and shipping lanes of all sunken craft and other debris, so the *Hellespont* was raised, towed out to sea and sunk off Grand Harbour, where she now sits upright and is completely embedded in the seabed. Her stern is intact and her rudder can still be seen, but her propeller is under the silt and rocks. One of her boilers lies off to the side and both paddle wheels have long since disintegrated; however the paddle wheel drive shafts are still intact. A large capstan has now collapsed through the rotten, wooden aft decks and the entire wreck is now a mess of confusion as it slowly settles and comes apart. Old fishing lines and some nets are snagged on the superstructure, and care, as always, should be taken when diving old wrecks at such a depth.

2 MV ODILE
★★

Location: In Kalkara Creek directly between Vittoriosa and Kalkara.
Access: Drive via Vittoriosa Quay and tunnel to the creek. Park next to the swings, with entry from the wall; swim out in line with the old lift shaft on the far side; the wreck is mid-channel.
Conditions: Fairly sheltered in the inner creek off the Grand Harbour, though visibility will drop to zero if you disturb the fine layer of silt which lies over everything.
Average depth: 20m (66ft)
Maximum depth: 24m (77ft)
Average visibility: 6m (20ft)

Originally thought to be the wreck of HMS *Abingdon*, sunk on 4 April 1942, the wreck is actually that of the Italian steam freighter MV *Odile*, which was bombed during World War II, then 'salvaged' in the 1970s. Fairly well broken up (the bows and the propeller are missing), facing northwest and lying on her port side, the wreck covers a large area and is difficult to find in poor visibility without local knowledge. Penetration of the wreck is possible, but only for very experienced divers with the proper equipment (including reels). You can swim the entire wreck in 40 minutes. This is a good dive when the northwesterly winds spoil the other side of the island.

3 HMS JERSEY
★★

Location: Entrance to Grand Harbour.
Access: Through Kalkara to the wartime buildings below Fort Ricasola (reached via the footpath from the car park at the fort).
Conditions: Beware large passing ships and marine traffic. The site is exposed to northeasterly swells and wind.
Average depth: 13–15m (43–50ft)
Maximum depth: 18m (60ft)
Average visibility: 6–10m (20–33ft)
Enter the water near the buildings at the water's edge, swim to the near end of the breakwater on the surface, about 100m (330ft), then submerge and follow the due north setting on your compass for about 30 minutes. The seabed is mainly flat sand and rubble, though with some interesting boulders and marine life. The *Jersey* itself hit a mine and sank as she was entering Grand Harbour; the remains of the bow section are all that is left.

4 THE SUBMARINE PEN
★★

Location: On the corner north of the fish market at Valletta, Grand Harbour.
Access: From the steps in front of the fish market with a

ENVIRONMENTAL PROTECTION

To avoid causing inadvertent damage to the marine environment, it is important that divers observe the following rules:

- Avoid touching delicate marine organisms with hands, fins, tanks etc.
- Do not collect any marine life.
- Avoid overweighting and work on buoyancy control.
- Do not feed the fish alien foods harmful to them.
- Ensure that your equipment consoles do not drag on the reef.
- Do not use spear guns.
- Do not molest marine life, such as sea urchins.

FLOUNDERS [*BARBUN*]

Relatively common sand dwellers found in Maltese waters are wide-eyed flounders (*Bothus podas*) and turbot (*Psetta maxima*), which are skittish when approached and take off over the sand planes at great speed. Although they are found on *Posidonia* beds, they prefer white sandy seabeds such as in sheltered bays, where, with a flick of their tail, they are able to cover themselves in sand, leaving only the stalked eyes visible. Both species are regular prey for dolphins.

---

surface swim of around 90m (100yd).
Conditions: Fairly sheltered, with visibility variable over a rock and weed substrate.
Average depth: 10m (33ft)
Maximum depth: 18m (60ft)
Average visibility: 6m (20ft)
During World War II a rough cutting in the rocks here was proposed as a submarine pen, but the project was abandoned. Torches are recommended on this dive to explore the cut and various crevices, now home to seahorses (*Hippocampus ramulosus*), shannies (*Lipophrys pholis*), triplefin blennies (*Tripterygion xanthosoma*) and various scorpionfish. The seabed is littered with war debris.

5 HMS MAORI
★★★

Location: In front of the café at the entrance to the dockyard creek at St Elmo's Bay.
Access: From the slippery steps and concrete walkway in front of the café, 120m (400ft) north and a 5min swim before descending onto the wreck at the edge of the drop.
Conditions: Fairly sheltered, but visibility is a problem, especially during easterly storms.
Average depth: 13m (43ft)
Maximum depth: 18m (60ft)
Average visibility: 6m (20ft)
HMS *Maori* was launched in 1937 and saw considerable action in the Norwegian campaign, Atlantic convoys and the Mediterranean. She was ultimately responsible for sinking the *Bismarck* and picked up a number of her survivors; while en route from Gibraltar the *Maori* was also involved in a successful attack against an Italian flotilla. However, ships at berth in Malta's harbours were always at risk from aerial attacks launched from airfields in Libya. On the night of 12 February 1942 the *Maori* received a direct hit in her engine room and the ship slowly began to sink. Declared a hazard to navigation she was subsequently 'cleared', her guns being removed and the ship wrecked. The bows and the entire stern are gone, but part of the raised bridge is still there and, from the rear, divers are able to gain relatively safe and

easy access to her remains, with exits through the large holes in her starboard side. There are still live shells protruding from the wreckage and mud, which should not be touched. Although she is silted up, the *Maori* is home to large numbers of fish, and the rocky slope has some interesting nudibranchs and octopuses amongst the algae and tube worms.

6 X131 LIGHTER (CAROLITA BARGE)
★★

Location: At the start of Lazzaretto Creek and opposite the old hospital on Manoel Island in Marsamxett harbour.
Access: From the shore next to the dogs' home or from the steps before you get to the Royal Malta Yacht Club.
Conditions: Fairly sheltered in the harbour, but suffers from easterly storms and high rainfall, reducing the underwater visibility to almost nil.
Average depth: 12m (40ft)
Maximum depth: 22m (73ft)
Average visibility: 6m (20ft)
Previously mistaken for a submarine, this wreck is actually of the X131 Lighter, *Carolita*. One of 200 vessels built for the Gallipoli Campaign and designed by Walter Pollocks and Sons of Faversham in Kent. The 160 ton

HMS Maori (Site 5) can easily be accessed by divers from the shore.

X131 took part in the Dardanelles Campaign and finally ended up in Malta in 1921 when she was converted into a water carrier. She received a torpedo hit to her stern on the night of 21 April 1942 and sunk immediately. Her bows are now in 6m (20ft) of water and the rear of the ship is at 22m (73ft). The deck of this water barge is flat and there are two hatches up front (with restricted access); access to the engine room is from beneath the bridge or in through the damaged stern. Large friendly striped grouper (*Epinephelus alexandrinus*) are found at the stern. On the swim back to the exit point you will find further remnants from the war days, in the shape of a typewriter, beds and other oddities discarded from the nearby old hospital. There are chromis and a few octopuses around, but this is generally a training dive and the site is always busy with divers.

7 THE TENT PEG WRECK
★★

Location: In Marsamxett harbour, southwest of the barge *Carolita* (Site 6).
Access: Either by swimming southwest from the *Carolita* or directly out from Ta' Xbiex seafront.
Conditions: Fairly sheltered but visibility is a problem.
Average depth: 20–25m (66–80ft)
Maximum depth: 27m (90ft)
Average visibility: 4m (13ft)

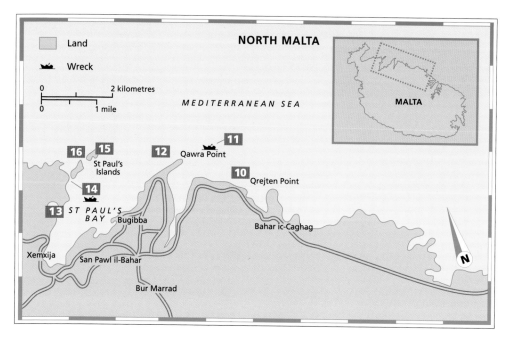

The seabed is composed of undulating fine white sand and silt. The wreck, formerly a steel cargo steamer, lies in a small valley and is very broken up; she was carrying a general cargo, including wooden tent pegs. The general marine life in the area is surprisingly profuse, with weaverfish (*Trachinus draco*), flounders (*Bothus podas*) and striped mullet (*Mullus surmuletus*).

8 THE SWIMMING POOL

★★★

Location: Off the sea-water swimming pool at the club in front of the Preluna Hotel in Sliema.
Access: Permission must be obtained from the club. Access is from the left-hand corner of the sea wall, with a giant stride entry.
Conditions: Fairly exposed, but generally an easy dive, perfect for trainee divers.
Average depth: 8m (27ft)
Maximum depth: 12m (40ft)
Average visibility: 12m (40ft)
The reef gently slopes out to the north, with various shallow undercuts where small fish can be found. This is a favourite site for local (illegal) spearfishermen, so do not expect to see any large fish. On the return to the outer wall of the swimming pool at the eastern corner you will come across a large, very narrow natural arch, with a tangle of old steel reinforcing cable and concrete in front of it. Exit is by climbing the rickety ladder on the outer wall of the pool.

9 BEAUFIGHTER 'N'

★★★

Location: 900m (1000yds) offshore, northwest of St Julian's Point, directly opposite Dive Systems.
Access: By boat only.
Conditions: Exposed site, so it can be choppy with some current.
Average depth: 35m (125ft)
Maximum depth: 38m (128ft)
Average visibility: 12m (40ft)
The Beaufighter 'N' was just one of many aeroplanes lost in the protection of these islands during World War II. Used to accompany the Bristol Beaufort torpedo on bombing raids on enemy shipping, this Beaufighter, with others from No. 272 Squadron, was leaving Malta on 17 March 1943, to escort 9 Beaufort Bombers for another torpedo bombing run to Point Stelo. Commanded by Sgt. Donald Frazee, with Sgt. Sandray as observer, the aircraft developed

---

HMS STUBBORN

Approximately 4.5km (2½ miles) north of Qawra Point lies HMS *Stubborn*, a British submarine built in Birkenhead. Sunk as an ASDIC checkpoint target for the British Navy's sonar signals, she sits almost upright in 60m (200ft) of water. Visibility is generally good, as it is so far out to sea, but this dive is only for very experienced divers and penetration of the wreck is not advisable.

mechanical problems soon after take off. It started to vibrate rapidly and quickly began to lose altitude. Unable to reach the safety of the airfield, the crew had no alternative but to ditch the fighter into the sea. They struck at over 100mph. Thankfully both crew escaped the wreck, which apparently stayed afloat only about 15 seconds. They were picked up by Maltese *dghajsas* before further help arrived. The aircraft now lies upside down on a clean sandy seabed, nearby a telecommunications cable. Much of the underside of the fuselage has rotted away and much else of the aeroplane is buried under the sand. However both wings are still fairly intact and both the undercarriage frames and now shredded tyres stick up from their wing positions behind the engines. The port starboard engine cowling is gone, with the propeller partly buried except for one blade which stands upright, the starboard propeller broke off during impact and now lies around 30m (100ft) away from the aircraft. Divers are able to inspect the undercarriage and machine gun assemblies that are covered in a fine patina of marine growth. The wreck site is surrounded by thousands of chromis.

10 GHALLIS ROCK
★★★

Location: Off the northern coast along the coast road between Sliema and Bugibba. Past the tower on Qrejten Point, the rocks are about 100m (330ft) offshore.
Access: By boat, but can be done from the rocky shore.
Conditions: Quite exposed, but sheltered from the northwesterly *Majjistral*. Boat traffic is intense in the shallower areas, so extra vigilance should be taken.
Average depth: 8m (27ft)
Maximum depth: 14m (47ft)
Average visibility: 15m (50ft)
This is an easy novice dive over and around some boulders with lots of *Posidonia* sea grass beds. The boulders are covered in algae, where striped mullet (*Mullus sermuletus*) and two-banded bream (*Diplodus vulgaris*) can be seen feeding, in addition to all the wrasse species.

11 WRECK IMPERIAL EAGLE
★★★

Location: Offshore between Qawra Point and Qrejten Point.
Access: By boat only.
Conditions: Exposed site, so it can be choppy with some current.
Average depth: 28m (95ft)
Maximum depth: 42m (140ft)

Average visibility: 25m (80ft)
The *Imperial Eagle* was a former ferry and cargo ship operating between Gozo and Malta. She is 45m (150ft) long with a beam of 9m (30ft) and was finally sunk as an artificial reef and proposed conservation area on 19 July 1999. Unfortunately, the Government have still failed to act in creating this conservation area, but it is hoped for the future. This site is regarded as a long deep dive in an undersea valley. First stop is the 'Christ Statue' in 25m (80ft), then proceed down the valley to the bows of the ship. Sitting intact and upright and relatively new, her spoked steering wheel is quite photogenic. She has a fine patina of algae and is home to many wrasse, chromis, bogue and grouper. The sides of the surrounding underwater valley are covered in *Posidonia*.

12 QAWRA REEF
★★★★

Location: 500m (¹/₃ mile) off the northwest tip of Qawra Point.
Access: By boat only and local knowledge is necessary.
Conditions: Very exposed; can be choppy with current.
Average depth: 25m (80ft)
Maximum depth: 50m (165ft)
Average visibility: Beyond 30m (100ft)
The dive boat is able to anchor on the reef lip in around 12m (40ft). As you drop over the algae-covered rocks there are five big caves to explore, indented about 10–12m (33–40ft) into the rocky wall. The caverns are all safe for divers and the walls are covered in sea rose algae (*Pseudolithophyllum expansum*) and sea lace bryozoan (*Reteporella septentrionalis*). The marine goldfish (*Anthias anthias*), considered quite rare around the islands, can be found in these offshore caverns.

13 MISTRA BAY
★★★

Location: In the western part of St Paul's Bay.
Access: Off the beach.
Conditions: Sheltered from the winter *Majjistral*, but can be busy with swimmers and boat traffic.
Average depth: 5m (17ft)
Maximum depth: 10m (33ft)
Average visibility: 6m (20ft)
A beginners' dive site when bad weather spoils Marfa Point, this is a shallow *Posidonia* grass bed inshore from a French-owned commercial fish farm. There is a lot of pollution in the area as a result, but the depth and conditions make it perfect for checkout dives and training.

The deep-water trench between western Sicily and Malta is now thought to have possibly the second largest population of great white sharks in the world. *Carcharodon carcharias* is the ocean's ultimate eating machine and attacks by these reputed man-eaters numbered about five a year throughout the Mediterranean in the 1950s and 1960s.

A great white shark has been caught in a fisherman's net as far away as the Black Sea, having negotiated both the narrow straits at Çanakkale and the Bosphorus. The last fatality took place near the island of Elba in 1989, whilst a more recent incident was in 1998 when a great white attacked a 6m (20ft) cabin cruiser 12 miles off the Italian Adriatic coast. The World Conservation Union has discovered that most of the sightings fall within a rough triangle stretching between Sicily, Malta and Cap Bon of Tunisia; unfortunately for the

sharks, their population appears to be dwindling because of the reduction in stocks of tuna, their main food source.

SHARK CATCHES

Great white sharks first gained notoriety in Malta in 1956 when Jack Smedley, a technical teacher working for the British Navy, was killed off St Thomas Bay. His body was never recovered. Although stories were bandied about for many years, it wasn't until 1964 and more particularly in 1973 that great white sharks received real media attention, when news came of a 5.5m (18ft) specimen being landed in Malta. The fisherman was Alfredo Cutajar and, at the time, this was the largest shark caught in the Mediterranean.

Alfredo became something of a local celebrity after this. In 1977 he caught a 7m (23ft) monster great white so large it would not fit in his boat. This shark was recorded as the largest great white shark ever landed complete in the world, and Alfredo, thereafter known locally as the 'Son of God', was reckoned to be a shark magnet. Photographs at the time show Alfredo placing his head in the mouth of the dead shark, which could once easily have eaten him whole. Later, Alfredo went on to make another record, catching a requiem shark – extremely rare in the Mediterranean and never before found in Maltese waters.

John Abela, a local shark-monitoring expert with the European Shark Research Bureau, said that Alfredo's record-breaking great white shark was a female aged between 25 and 30 years old, had recently been pregnant with nine pups, and was ravenous after her long pregnancy. Travelling with her mate, the shark became entangled in Alfredo's fishing cables. When she was winched ashore at Marsaxlokk and cut open, she was found to contain a 2m (6ft) dolphin, a 2m (6ft) blue shark and a turtle.

GREAT WHITES IN RETREAT
Baby great whites have been caught in Maltese waters since then, and both males and females are caught regularly off Tunisia, but these reports are becoming rarer. The sharks increasingly tend to live in deeper offshore locations where it is thought they now prey on dolphins, also an open water species. Great white sharks are considered so rare that you are highly unlikely to see any while diving.

Recently, an international campaign has been launched to help protect sharks and

Opposite: *A record-breaking 7m (23ft) great white was caught by Alfredo Cutajar in 1977.*
Above: *The great white shark remains the world's ultimate predator.*

promote the study of them. For details contact: The Shark Trust, 36 Kingfisher Court, Hambridge Rd, Newbury, Berks RG14 5SJ, UK, tel (+44) (0)1635 550 380/fax (+44) (0)1635 550 230, e-mail: sharktrust@naturebureau.co.uk; http://ds.dial.pipex.com/sharktrust/

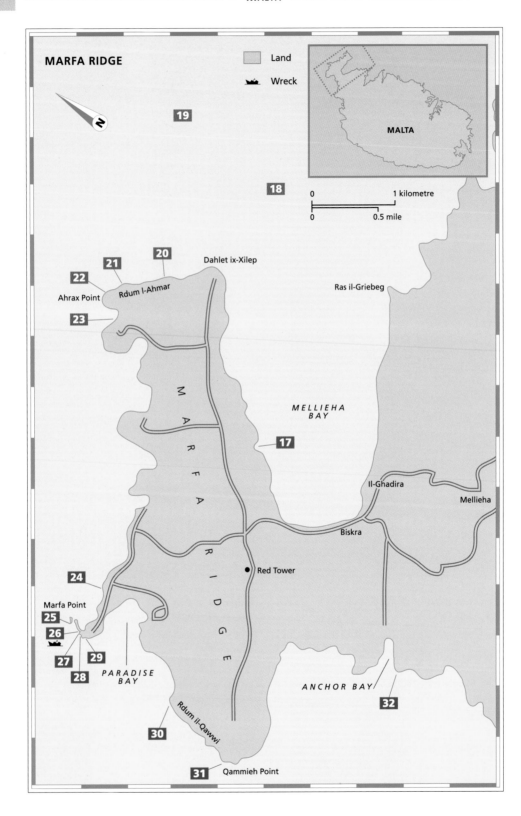

MARFA RIDGE

Land

Wreck

MALTA

19

18

0   1 kilometre

0   0.5 mile

20

21

22

Ahrax Point   Rdum l-Ahmar

23

Dahlet ix-Xilep

Ras il-Griebeg

M A R F A

MELLIEHA
BAY

17

Il-Ghadira

Mellieha

Biskra

R I D G E

24

Red Tower

Marfa Point

25

26

27   29

28

PARADISE
BAY

ANCHOR BAY

32

Rdum il-Qawwi

30

31   Qammieh Point

14 ST PAUL'S WRECK

★★★★

Location: On the inside of the St Paul's islands between the inner island and the shore.
Access: By boat or from the shore, although a four-wheel-drive vehicle is required for the rough access road.
Conditions: Fairly sheltered from the northwest winds, but can be choppy with surge.
Average depth: 6m (20ft)
Maximum depth: 12m (40ft)
Average visibility: 12m (40ft)

This is reputed to be the location where St Paul was wrecked. Although nothing remains of his biblical wooden ship, there are several other remains, including some plates and ribs from an old destroyer in shallow water and a small ferry sunk by Captain Morgan in 1984 for his glass-bottomed boat trips. An algae-covered statue of Christ with outstretched arms is also to be found in the area, though it is rather difficult to locate. The seabed is covered in *Posidonia* with sand patches in between.

15 OCTOPUS'S GARDEN
(ST PAUL'S REEF)

★★

Location: 5min by boat from St Paul's harbour, to the east of outer St Paul's Island.
Access: By boat.
Conditions: Fairly sheltered from the northwest winds, but otherwise rather exposed and can be choppy with surface surge.
Average depth: 7m (24ft)
Maximum depth: 25m (80ft)

MORAY EELS [*MORINA*] AND CONGER EELS [*GRINGU*]

Moray eels (*Muraena helena*) are fairly common around all the reefs, but relatively timid and mostly seen at night. They live in cracks in the deep reefs and around wrecks. Not to be confused with conger eels (which have a long dorsal fin), Mediterranean moray eels have a beautiful golden pattern on their bodies, variable in extent and ranging from small spots around the head to great vertical bands and golden blotches.

Conger eels (*Conger conger*) live in wrecks and caverns and under overhangs. Fairly inquisitive, and very sociable, they are liable to come out and look at you if you get too close. Conger eels are recorded all over the Mediterranean, as well as from the Black Sea right up to Iceland and as far west as the Azores. Active night predators, they grow to over 3m (10ft) in length and can appear threatening. They are dull grey in colour.

Average visibility: 12m (40ft)

This is an open water reef dive. The algae-covered bedrock and boulders create a mini-wall with a steep slope. Fish life is sparse as the area is popular with local fishermen, but there are numbers of small sea urchins and fireworms (*Hermodice carunculata*). The fireworms are voracious predators and scavengers, cleaning up dead and decaying sea urchins, jellyfish, corals etc.

16 ST PAUL'S VALLEY

★★★

Location: Between the two St Paul's islands and to the northwest part of the channel.
Access: By boat.
Conditions: Can be choppy with strong current running from the northwest between the islands.
Average depth: 12m (40ft)
Maximum depth: 25m (80ft)
Average visibility: 12m (40ft)

The boat anchors at the edge of the drop-off in 6m (20ft); there is a short swim to the mini-wall, which drops another 3m (10ft) to the white sandy seabed. This is interspersed with boulders and raised banks of *Posidonia*, where cuttlefish and numerous wrasse can be found. Pay close attention to the sea grass as you should be able to find the broad-snouted pipefish (*Sygnathus phlegon*). Small gobies inhabit the interface between the algae and sand patches, where sand divers (*Synodus saurus*) are also common.

17 SLUG'S BAY

★★★

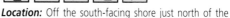

Location: Off the south-facing shore just north of the Mellieha Bay Hotel in Mellieha Bay.
Access: From the shore.
Conditions: Fairly sheltered from northerly winds, but can be totally blown out with zero visibility when the wind is from the southeast.
Average depth: 4m (14ft)
Maximum depth: 8m (27ft)
Average visibility: 15m (20ft)

This site is used mainly by Aquaventure for training purposes and is the first introduction many divers get to the Mediterranean. There is enough diversity in the area to make this site attractive and also interesting at night. The shallows are covered by stones and *Posidonia*, and there are large numbers of octopuses. To the left (east) is a small archway; continuing from here is a cavern which has some interesting fish and invertebrates. Moray eels can be found as well as large numbers of chromis (*Chromis chromis*).

BRYOZOANS

Bryozoans are often mistaken for a species of coral. False coral (*Myriapora truncata*) is very common in Maltese caves, caverns and any other area that is predominantly shaded, such as some of the vertical clefts and cliffs on the northwest coasts. Ranging from orange to dark red in colour, bryozoans resemble true branching corals and are easily broken. One of the most delicate is the sea lace bryozoan (*Reteporella septentrionalis*), which can be dislodged by exhaled air bubbles. Divers should enter caves and caverns only infrequently, as trapped air resulting from large numbers of divers visiting the same area can kill off the animals that live on the ceiling.

18 GURBEL REEF

★★★

Location: Directly out of Mellieha Bay, between Dahlet ix-Xilep and Ras il-Griebeg, about 5min by boat.
Access: By boat.
Conditions: Fairly exposed and can be choppy with surge present.
Average depth: 15m (50ft)
Maximum depth: 25m (80ft)
Average visibility: 15m (50ft)
This offshore reef takes its name from the Maltese word for the brown meagre (*Argyrosomus regius*), which is found here in large numbers. There are some striking and unusual rock formations amidst a tumble of large and small boulders, all of which are covered in a profusion of algae. Red scorpionfish (*Scorpaena scrofa*) are common, as are cardinalfish (*Apogon imberbis*), striped mullet (*Mullus surmuletus*) and salema (*Sarpa salpa*).

19 THE WHITE REEF (HOOFER'S REEF)

★★★★

Location: 2.5km (1¹/₂ miles) northeast of Rdum L-Ahmar, the easterly side of the Marfa Ridge, to a raised reef called Sikka I-Bajda (The White Reef).
Access: By boat only.
Conditions: Exposed offshore reef, with surge and surface chop to be expected, along with light current. Rarely dived.
Average depth: 15m (50ft)
Maximum depth: 25m (80ft), though over 70m (230ft) beyond the drop-off
Average visibility: 30m (100ft)
This offshore reef, which rises to within 12m (40ft) of the surface, is a massive rocky ridge that has hardly been explored. Located too far out for most smaller fishing boats to access, there are large numbers of amberjack, bream, parrotfish and grouper to be found here. The reef also has a profusion of spiny starfish (*Marthasterias glacialis*) and featherstarfish (*Antedon mediterranea*).

20 SMUGGLER'S COVE

★★★★★

Location: Off the eastern point of the Marfa Ridge.
Access: By boat.
Conditions: Fairly sheltered from northwesterly winds.
Average depth: 6m (20ft)
Maximum depth: 15m (50ft)
Average visibility: 15m (50ft)
Named by Aquaventure, this is a nice easy dive onto a flat sandy seabed interspersed with rocks and *Posidonia* banks. As you swim further out to sea, the seabed becomes strewn with much larger algae-covered boulders, with sea urchins, starfish and fireworms everywhere. On the inshore side, there is a large cavern at 3m (10ft), which opens out with a small swimthrough at the rear. There are lots of chromis all over this area, as well as several species of bream, sand smelt and parrotfish.

21 RDUN L-AHMAR (RED CLIFFS)

★★★★

Location: Near Ahrax Point.
Access: Drive down to Ahrax Bay, turning right and driving up the hill (four-wheel-drive recommended). Walk due east to a small patch of weedy rock after about 90m (100yd) of needle-sharp rocks and crevices.
Conditions: Exposed location, but worth the effort. Be careful of local boat traffic in the summer months.
Average depth: 25–35m (80–115ft)
Maximum depth: 36m (120ft)
Average visibility: Beyond 30m (100ft)
Very rarely dived due to difficult access, this site has large numbers of massive rocks and boulders creating swimthroughs. Larger pelagic fish are often encountered here, including amberjacks (*Seriola dumerili*) and eagle rays (*Myliobatis aquila*). Grouper can be found in deeper waters where the boulders give way to rubble and sand.

22 DRAGONARA CAVE (CORAL GROTTO) (AHRAX POINT)

★★★★★

Location: Off the northwest point of the Marfa Ridge.
Access: By boat, but can be reached from the shore, although it is a long and rough walk.
Conditions: Fairly sheltered in the main cavern, but strong surge when the weather is from the southeast.

Above: *Colourful scorpionfish such as this Scorpaena notata live on the shallow reefs.*

Average depth: 7m (24ft)
Maximum depth: 18m (60ft)
Average visibility: 30m (100ft)

This is a popular dive with photographers as there are some lovely scenic views from inside the caverns, looking out to sea. The boat anchors in around 10m (33ft) and then it is a short swim to the outside cavern. From here a tunnel at 5–7m (17–24ft) opens up into a small inland grotto, open to daylight. As it is almost completely landlocked, the water temperature in here is often a few degrees higher than outside, allowing for increased coral growth with an abundance of golden cup corals (*Astroides calycularis*), false coral (*Myriapora truncata*) and many different types of tube worm and starfish.

This is a lovely bay with a variety of habitats to suit most tastes. There are numerous gullies cut into the limestone as you swim east (to the right). Turning the corner you drop into a large cauldron-shaped depression in the bedrock, with a blow hole on the inside where it is possible to surface. If you continue to the right, the wall starts to shelve steeply to over 30m (100ft). Back inside the shelter of the bay, the algae-covered bedrock gives way to *Posidonia* and then to gravel and fine sand where it is possible to see flying gurnards (*Dactylopterus volitans*) and even stargazers (*Uranoscopus scaber*). The usual large numbers of saddled bream (*Oblada melanura*) and green wrasse (*Labrus viridis*) can be found amongst the algae.

23 AHRAX BAY
★★★

Location: Off the northeastern shore.
Access: Popular as a shore dive, but can be done by boat.
Conditions: Fairly sheltered, but can be choppy with some surge.
Average depth: 9m (30ft)
Maximum depth: 25m (80ft)
Average visibility: 30m (100ft)

24 MARFA BAY
★★★

Location: Off the northern shore of the Marfa Ridge, near some fishermen's cottages and a slipway.
Access: From the shore to the right of the slipway and over some large boulders.
Conditions: Sheltered from the worst of the weather.

Average depth: 3m (10ft)
Maximum depth: 6m (20ft)
Average visibility: 12m (40ft)
This is a very easy dive after a brief scramble over the rocks. Large *Posidonia* banks result in dead grass debris collecting amidst the smooth limestone gullies. There are hundreds of snakelocks anemones (*Anemonia viridis*) and, if you look closely, you will see several species of goby, as well as the spider crab found accompanying the anemones. Hermit crabs are common, as are sea urchins and small starfish. The area is popular locally for swimming and snorkelling.

25 CIRKEWWA ARCH
★★★

Location: Off the west side of the harbour wall at the Cirkewwa ferry terminal.
Access: From the shore, either at the old steel jetty or from the wall entrance and a jump into the water.
Conditions: Sheltered from the southeast winds, but can be choppy with current to be expected.
Average depth: 15m (50ft)
Maximum depth: 36m (120ft)
Average visibility: 30m (100ft)
This archway is seldom dived as most divers tend to focus on the *Rozi* (Site 26) or concentrate on easier dives in the area. The arch is located along the edge of the protective reef and is set back from the drop-off. It is essentially a cavern which has a large hole in the top, creating a narrow bridge of rock under which divers can easily gain access. The arch is the highlight of the dive as the rest of the reef is made up of a thick algae fuzz and *Posidonia* beds.

26 THE TUGBOAT ROZI
★★★★

Location: Approximately 120m (400ft) directly out from the old steel jetty on a bearing of 280° magnetic.

JACKS [*SAWRELLA*]

Amberjacks (*Seriola dumerili*) [*Accjola*] are very common and often seen in small hunting groups darting in amongst the chromis and sand smelt. Bonito (*Sarda sarda*) [*Plamtu*] are found in deeper water and offshore reefs, where they round up and attack shoals of sardines. Known locally as *lampuka*, the dolphinfish (*Coryphaena hippurus*) features regularly on Maltese menus from September to January, when large schools of this fast-moving fish visit the waters surrounding the islands. Dolphinfish are attracted to fishing areas by large floats which cast a shadow into the water. The fish like to hide under this shadow and, once enough fish are sighted, they are caught by means of a purse seine net.

Access: By jumping into the water next to the old steel pier and swimming out on the surface.
Conditions: Fairly sheltered from the northeast winds, but can be choppy with strong current.
Average depth: 30m (100ft)
Maximum depth: 36m (120ft)
Average visibility: 30m (100ft)
The *Rozi* was sunk in 1992 as an underwater attraction for tourists on submarine tours. These trips no longer operate, but this wonderful little tugboat continues to sit upright on a sandy bottom within a rocky amphitheatre. The ship is slowly being colonized and all areas are accessible. Around the ship are thousands of fish, with chromis, bream and sand smelt predominating. Also amberjack (*Seriola dumerili*) and bonito (*Sarda sarda*), which 'buzz' the shoals of small fish. The flat sandy seabed around the wreck is covered in huge anemones (*Condylactis aurantica*). Leave the wreck and swim towards the shore, past a large anchor partially embedded in the sand, until you reach the sloping wall, where the first of a few small tunnels eventually lead to the Marfa Point entry.

27 CIRKEWWA POINT (MARFA POINT) (THE MADONNA)
★★★★★

Location: Directly out from the Marfa Point entry and down the corner of the wall to 18m (60ft).
Access: From the shore.
Conditions: Always busy and fairly sheltered from the northeast winds, but can be choppy.
Average depth: 12m (40ft)
Maximum depth: 18m (60ft)
Average visibility: 18m (60ft)
A statue of the Madonna, placed here by the Amphibians Diving Club, sits in a small natural cavern in 18m (60ft) of water. The rocks in the area are covered in numerous fireworms (*Hermodice carunculata*), all entwined as they eat small sea urchins and jellyfish. As you continue toward the point from the statue, there are attractive overhangs covered in golden zoanthids (*Parazoanthus axinellae*). These lead to a largish swimthrough, all the way through the head. There are a few octopuses in the shallows.

28 CIRKEWWA (MARFA CENTRAL) (THE TRAINING POOL)
★★★★★

Location: Out from Marfa Point entry and to the left.
Access: From the shore.
Conditions: Very busy but fairly sheltered from the northeast winds.
Average depth: 6m (20ft)

Maximum depth: 18m (60ft)
Average visibility: 18m (60ft)
This is by far the easiest shore diving site in the area, with convenient access down a concrete ramp to the water's edge and into 1m (3ft) of water. A short swim takes you into the first of two small valleys between the rocky reefs, where much of the dive training takes place. If you continue to your left and out to sea, you reach the edge of the wall with a large overhanging shelf where great numbers of cardinalfish (*Apogon imberbis*) congregate. Continue around this headland and, near the next corner on your right, you will find a horizontal fissure where moray eels (*Muraena helena*) and coral shrimps (*Stenopus spinosus*) can be seen. This fissure runs towards a large cavern with four narrow exits, which is very photogenic.

29 PARADISE BAY
★★★★★

Location: Off the southwestern end of Marfa Point and the headland in front of the south jetty.
Access: From the shore.

The tugboat Rozi, deliberately sunk in 1992, now acts as a magnet for divers (Site 26).

Conditions: Sheltered from the northeast winds, but there can be surge on the entry point, so divers are encouraged to exit at the Marfa Point entry.
Average depth: 6m (20ft)
Maximum depth: 18m (60ft)
Average visibility: 18m (60ft)
There is a hard walk over sharp fossilized rock south of the car park. The shoreline by the harbour wall is rocky, with pools of stagnant water, but once in the sea the rocky reef falls away amidst a tumble of *Posidonia*-covered boulders. The dive continues around the headland to the right (north) and follows the edge of the wall. The shallows are filled with thousands of juvenile chromis and sand smelt.

30 RDUN IL-QAWWI (ROUGH CLIFFS)
★★★★★

Location: North of Qammieh Point.
Access: Along the road behind the Red Tower and park at

the end at the top of the cliffs, with steps and footpath for over 500m (550yd). Entry is from the slipway in the lagoon.
Conditions: Fairly sheltered from the northeast winds, but blown out during northwesterlies.
Average depth: 6–40m (20–130ft)
Maximum depth: 45m (150ft)
Average visibility: 30m (100ft)
This site features dozens of small swimthroughs under the masses of boulders that litter the shore. Here are golden zoanthids (*Parazoanthus axinellae*) and various sponges, while the *Posidonia* 'meadows' are filled with small wrasse. The bay eventually drops down to sand fields at 38m (124ft). This dive is worth the climb, especially for the arches and caves along the shoreline at 0–10m (0–33ft), but the route there can be slippery after rain.

31 DEVIL'S REEF
★★★★

Location: Off the southwestern point of Qammieh Point at the western end of Marfa.
Access: By boat.
Conditions: Fairly sheltered from the northeast winds, but can be choppy with strong current.
Average depth: 30m (100ft)
Maximum depth: Beyond 70m (230ft)
Average visibility: 30m (100ft)

Schools of sand smelt and chromis are a particularly common sight.

This is an exciting dive off the reef that juts out southwest from Qammieh Point to a couple of small islands just offshore. Similar in feel to Reqqa Point on Gozo (Site 5), this reef drops near vertically to the seabed 50m (165ft) below and then slopes off to very deep water. On the southern side of the wall is an ancient cave with clear signs of stalactites, now completely submerged. This is a popular place for sightings of predatory fish such as barracuda (*Sphyraena sphyraena*), dentex (*Dentex dentex)*, amberjack (*Seriola dumerili*) and even Crevalle jacks (*Caranx hippos*).

32 ANCHOR BAY / POPEYE VILLAGE
★★★★

Location: Off the southern edge of the new pier in Anchor Bay, opposite the Popeye Village.
Access: From the shore.
Conditions: The bay is quite sheltered but has very poor visibility. However, the clarity improves near the entrance to the cave around the corner to your left (south).
Average depth: 6m (20ft)
Maximum depth: 12m (40ft)
Average visibility: 12m (40ft)
The bay itself is rather dull, but once you head around the corner you come across a massive boulder next to the shoreline wall. This marks the entrance of the cave, which has a base of rounded stones. The right-hand wall is pitted with thousands of small holes where fireworms, shrimps and sea urchins live. The cave is sizeable, and you can duck

One of the reasons Malta has been at the forefront of Mediterranean diving for many years is the large number of wrecks in its waters, particularly those sunk as a direct result of military action during World War II. The British Navy made use of the islands' strategic location in planning its counter-attack of the Italian and German forces, and hoped to take advantage of the deep, safe, natural anchorage at Valletta.

There are a number of wrecks within the harbour confines of the Valletta area and most can be reached quite easily, for example HMS *Maori*, the barge *Carolita*, the 'Tent Peg Wreck', MV *Odile* and HMS *Jersey*. HMS *Maori* and the *Carolita* are the most accessible and are considered easy shore dives.

MALTA'S WRECKS

HMS *Maori* was sunk by enemy action on the night of 12 February 1942, though fortunately without loss of life. The wreck remained a navigational hazard for many years; eventually she was salvaged to a degree and her remains blasted to virtually seabed level. There are still live shells all around the hull. Divers can gain relatively safe access to HMS *Maori* either through the largely destroyed stern section or through the large holes in her starboard side. The interior of the ship is filled with soft sand and mud and divers should exercise great care to avoid stirring up the silt.

The barge *Carolita* is located in Marsamxett harbour, opposite the old naval hospital on Manoel Island, in a maximum depth of only 22m (73ft). The barge sank immediately after being hit in the stern by a German U-boat on the night of 21 April 1942. On the swim back to the exit point you will notice curious objects littering the seabed, all of them thrown out of the windows when the war hospital closed.

The MV *Odile* in Kalkara Creek was bombed during the war and 'salvaged' in the 1970s (the wreck was originally thought to be that of HMS *Abingdon*). While interesting, the wreck is fairly well broken up, and care should be taken to avoid the jagged metal parts which could snag diving equipment. Penetration of this shipwreck is not recommended.

HMS Maori was bombed in 1942 during a severe aerial attack on Malta.

These ships are all well documented, but there have been a few interesting recent finds, particularly military aircraft. There are the remains of a fairly well intact Blenheim Bomber to the south of the island, near Marsaxlokk and a Beaufighter, upside down and close to the shore, near St Julians. There is also the wreckage of an Italian Seaplane in the same vicinity.

There are some deep wrecks such as the HMS *Stubborn*, an intact submarine in 60m (200ft), *Le Polynesien* from World War I at the same depth; HMS *Southwold* in 70m (230ft) and the *Hellespont* from World War I and a World War II German E. Boat or 'Schnell Boot' in only 36m (140ft). These sites are now being visited more frequently as deep diving is now very much part of the Maltese diving scene.

The remains of many of these former vessels of war are now colonised by an amazing array of marine life, including tube worms, small schools of fish and tiny corals; all are fascinating to explore.

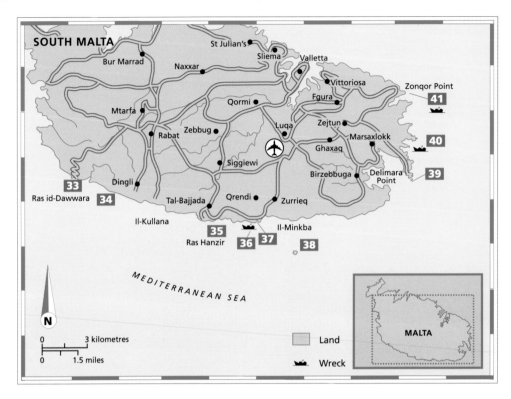

under a narrow lip and venture further into the cave and surface again before returning the same way. There are large numbers of brittle starfish and cave shrimps (*Palaemon serratus*), and in the spring the nudibranch *Hypselodoris elegans* is also found here.

33 M'TAHLEB
★★★★

Location: Off the east coast at the end of the road leading to Rdum tas-Sarg north of Ras id-Dawwara Bay.
Access: By boat, but can be done from the shore.

SHRIMPS [*GAMBLU*]

A relative of the tropical coral-banded shrimp (*Stenopus hispidus*) found in the Caribbean and Indo-Pacific, the Mediterranean banded shrimp (*Stenopus spinosus*) is one of those species commonly found on night dives, particularly around Marfa Point on Malta. It is a colourful small shrimp with long pincers and waving white antennae, which are what first attract your attention. They gather inside cavern entrances and clean up after conger and moray eels. The common shrimp (*Palaemon serratus*) is frequently found in large numbers in most caves, in particular the cave at Anchor Bay on Malta.

Conditions: A tough dive, with a long walk down from the only parking at the top of the hill, and entry and exit possible only in perfect sea conditions.
Average depth: 30m (100ft)
Maximum depth: Beyond 70m (230ft)
Average visibility: Beyond 30m (100ft)
This has remained a relatively unspoiled dive site on account of its inaccessibility – clambering down 300m (1000ft) of rugged headland may be manageable, but climbing back up after a deep dive is another matter. The site features vertical walls, ledges, caves and caverns with large numbers of wrasse, parrotfish, chromis and smelt. The algae here is home to a variety of fireworms, tube worms, hermit crabs, starfish and shrimps.

34 MIGRAH FERHA (HAPPY WELCOME) (THE STEPS)
★★★★★

Location: Off the Dingli Cliffs on the southwestern coast.
Access: By boat, or down a long and steep flight of 152 stone steps and rocks. Ensure that exit is possible before entering the water, as tidal swells can render it impossible.

The white-tipped Coryphella pedata is one of the most colourful of the Maltese nudibranchs.

CHROMIS [CAWLA]

Chromis belong to the family Pomacentridae. Extremely common around all of the Maltese islands, chromis (*Chromis chromis*) are small and oval in shape, and group together in large shoals, picking off plankton out of the water column. The juveniles are a royal blue in colour, but they gradually change to a dull greyish-green.

Conditions: Exposed, but sheltered from easterly winds.
Average depth: 40–60m (130–200ft)
Maximum depth: Beyond 60m (200ft)
Average visibility: 45m (150ft)

A spectacular wall dive with a climb that is difficult for the less fit. Entry is into 8m (27ft) of water, from where you head southeast. Along the wall is an archway and cave at 12m (40ft) which rises up inside to 4m (13ft), often with a layer of fresh water at the top. In the open water are barracuda, jacks, tuna and eagle rays. Very rarely dived, the vertical walls plummet underwater as far as they soar above. Large grouper (*Epinephelus guaza*) are common, as are comber (*Serranus cabrilla*) and all the species of wrasse and bream. Climb back up very slowly at the end of the dive. Count Roger the Norman invaded Malta here and called it 'Happy Welcome', so the climb can't be too bad!

35 GHAR LAPSI
★★★★★

Location: To the west of Ras Hanzir, off the south coast near the Mnajdra Temples.
Access: Entry from the shore with a ladder and giant stride entry point. The slipway is covered in algae and very slippery, and divers should take care here.
Conditions: Fairly sheltered from the northeast winds, but there can be poor visibility and surge in the cave when the weather is bad.
Average depth: 6m (20ft)
Maximum depth: 15m (50ft)
Average visibility: 12m (40ft)

A popular site with trainees, who can enter a safe, shallow cave that runs through the headland, starting in around 3m (10ft) and coming out on a convoluted wall at 6m (20ft) with a large pile of algae-covered boulders at the entrance. The cave has interesting sponges and bryozoans, including a tiny burrowing yellow sponge called *Cliona* and a stalked sponge (*Axinella verrucosa*). The outer areas of the cave have *Posidonia* and a variety of algae, all grazed on by wrasse and bream.

NUDIBRANCHS [*SERDUR IL-BAHAR*]

Rarely seen, nudibranchs or sea slugs are essentially molluscs which have lost their shells (their name means literally 'naked gill'), and they wear their exposed gills as a frondy appendage on their backs. Nudibranchs feed on a number of animals, particularly hydroids and small anemones, and are unharmed by their prey's stinging cells or nematocysts. Some species store the stinging cells in their own body as defence mechanisms. Nearly all are brightly coloured to warn predators that they are harmful. The flame nudibranch (*Flabelina affinis*) is vividly coloured and feeds on hydroids. The speckled nudibranch (*Hypselodoris valenciennesi*) is common on crustose algae mats.

---

36 WRECK UM EL FAROUD

★★★★★

Location: 140m (460ft) southwest of Wied iz-Zurrieq headland.
Access: From the shore or by boat.
Conditions: Sheltered from northeasterly winds, but exposed to other swells; current to be expected running from stern to bow.
Average depth: 25m (80ft)
Maximum depth: 34m (115ft)
Average visibility: 18m (60ft)
Sunk in September 1998, the *Um el Faroud* had previously lain in the harbour at Valletta for three years following an explosion on board that killed nine Maltese dockyard workers. Now, with a memorial brass plaque in place, the ship sits upright on a sandy seabed at 32m (108ft), the latest addition to Malta's artificial reef programme. At 10,000 tons and 110m (360ft) long the *Um el Faroud* is an impressive sight. The depth to the bridge is 15m (57ft) and the depth to the deck 25m (80ft). The wreck is completely open for penetration, but has not yet been made fully safe inside, and should only be attempted with proper training.

37 WIED IZ-ZURRIEQ (BLUE GROTTO)

★★★★★

Location: Off the ferry slip at Wied iz-Zurrieq headland for trips to the Blue Grotto.
Access: From the shore or by boat.
Conditions: Fairly sheltered from northeast winds, but can be blown out after heavy rainfall and southerly winds. Care should be taken with the amount of boat traffic overhead.
Average depth: 9m (30ft)
Maximum depth: 30m (100ft)
Average visibility: 25m (80ft)
Luzzus taking tourists around to the Blue Grotto ply this small bay. After a giant stride entry into the water, swim

across and out to the mouth of the bay and turn to your right (west) to follow the cliff wall. The first of the caves is on the corner at 23m (76ft); it has large numbers of cardinalfish (*Apogon imberbis*). The bigger cave (often called the Bell Cave or Chimney Cave) is just around the corner at about the same depth. It has three small entrances, one of which is fairly easy to negotiate. The interior walls are covered in sponges, tube worms, bryozoans and a few larger peacock worms. The exit is by retracing your route into the bay. Marine life over the algae beds includes cuttlefish and many species of wrasse.

38 FILFLA ISLAND

★★★★

Location: Off the southern shore.
Access: By boat.
Conditions: Fairly exposed from southerly swells. Expect the dive to be choppy with strong current.
Average depth: 25m (80ft)
Maximum depth: Beyond 70m (230ft)
Average visibility: Beyond 30m (100ft)
This site can be divided into several dives around the island. Once used for target practice during World War II, Filfla is now a National Nature Reserve and access is restricted. Diving is only possible with a special permit and numbers are limited, making this a dive that everyone wants to do. One or two dive centres, including the local BSAC branch, make regular visits. However, the waters surrounding the island are littered with armaments, and divers should exercise caution, making sure to avoid the munitions.

39 DELIMARA POINT

★★★★

Location: Off the southeastern point of Delimara past Marsaxlokk.
Access: By boat, but can be done from the old salt pans on the headland, although this is not recommended.
Conditions: Exposed and can be choppy with current; can only be dived when conditions are near perfect.
Average depth: 12m (40ft)
Maximum depth: 25m (80ft)
Average visibility: 18m (60ft)
Visibility at Delimara Point is often the clearest around the islands. This exposed site is at the extreme southeast tip, around the flat wedge-shaped rock off the headland. From here the wall drops down to around 12m (40ft), where you should be able to find a vertical fissure that drops to the seabed amongst some huge algae-covered boulders. Swimming from the base of the fissure to your left, you come to the entrance of a cave that leads up through a chimney to the reeftop. Parrotfish (*Sparisoma cretense*),

picarel (*Spicara smaris*) and large schools of chromis are quite common. The sides of the fissure have sea potatoes (*Halocinthya papillosa*) and lightbulb tunicates (*Clavelina nana*) as well as the spotted sea cucumber (*Holothuria forskali*) and purple sea urchins (*Sphaerechinus granularis*).

40 WRECK BRISTOL BLENHEIM
★★★

Location: 800m (870yd) due east of Xorb Il-Ghagin, off the southeast coast, in a depth of 41m (136ft).
Access: By boat only.
Conditions: Exposed, so can be choppy with current.
Average depth: 40m (130ft)
Maximum depth: 41.5m (136ft)
Average visibility: 15m (50ft)
On 13 December 1941, the Bristol Blenheim Mark IV of Number 18 Squadron was sent out on a bombing raid. The aircraft was quickly attacked after leaving Luqa airfield by an Italian Macchi. With her port engine disabled and port propeller shot off, the pilot Sgt. Frank Jury, accompanied by air-gunner Sgt. Dennis Mortimer and navigator Tom Black, decided to ditch the bomber over Marsaxlokk, after jettisoning her payload, near a *dghajsa* or Maltese fishing boat. All three crew escaped with little injury. The bomber is still lying upright but is deteriorating quite badly. Most of the central fuselage and both wings are still intact, but the tail and the cockpit are both gone. Her undercarriage is now exposed and you can see the

The Bristol Blenheim is located off southern Malta and is a popular site for divers.

intact starboard engine and propeller retracted inside the wing casings to aid her streamlined flight profile. The seabed is fairly clean with patches of *Posidonia* and the area abounds with small chromis and bogue.

41 WRECKS ST MICHAEL AND NUMBER 10
★★★

Location: Southeast of Zonqor Point, at the mouth of Marsascala Harbour.
Access: By boat.
Conditions: Sheltered from the northeast winds.
Average depth: 21m (70ft)
Maximum depth: 21m (70ft)
Average visibility: 18m (60ft)
These two tugboats, built in 1944, were scuttled in 1998 after having been given a full environmental clean-up. The *St Michael* is of Tanac type, 20m (66ft) long and built in Canada, while the *Number 10* is 16m (54ft) in length and of Melita type. Zonqor Point was chosen as the site partly on account of its clean, sandy seabed and absence of *Posidonia* sea grass meadows; the wrecks are expected to act as much needed artificial reefs. The Imperial Eagle Underwater Marine Park Committee have put together a monitoring programme to determine the speed of the marine growth and influx of fish to the area.

HOW TO GET THERE

By air: Air Malta flies from many countries, while Lufthansa, Swissair, Alitalia, Aeroflot, Balkan Airways and Tuninter also have regular flights. From the UK there are flights from Glasgow, Manchester, Birmingham, Dublin, London Heathrow (Terminal 4) and Gatwick, plus charter operations from Belfast, Cardiff, Bristol, Exeter, Newcastle, Leeds, Edinburgh and Aberdeen. There are also daily flights and charters from Rome, Frankfurt, Moscow and other European cities.
By sea: There are regular sailings to Malta from Italy and Libya. Operators include Sea Malta and Virtu Steamship Company.

GETTING AROUND

There are around 85 **car hire** companies on Malta; some have booths at the international airport. Costs are from Lm 8 per day, depending on season and the type of car, with special rates for one or two weeks. Many divers prefer the combi-van type of vehicle, especially when diving independently. **Alamo Car Hire**, tel (356) 21238745. **Avis Car Rental**, tel (356) 21235751. **Budget Rent-a-Car**, tel (356) 21241517. **Europcar**, tel (356) 21388516 (special rates in conjunction with Air Malta). **Hertz Car Rental**, tel (356) 21314636. **Westminster Car Rental**, tel (356) 21577172.

Malta has an extensive **bus** network. The main terminal is outside the City Gate in Valletta. **Taxis** can be found at the airport, at ferry terminals and around main hotels.

WHERE TO STAY

Most resort hotels have all the facilities you are likely to need, including restaurants, bars, nightclubs and sporting activities. As much of the coastline is rocky, there are few hotels on the beach, but the majority have sunbathing terraces or lidos and watersports facilities.

Eden Beach Hotel, St Augustine Rd, St George's Bay, STJ 06; tel (356) 21341191/ fax (356) 21341197; e-mail: ebeach@ maltanet.net. Situated next to a cinema and bowling alley, includes a superb health club, allied with the Westin Lido and Sports. **Grand Hotel Mercure San Antonio**, Triq it-Turisti, Qawra, SPB05; tel (356) 21583434/fax (356) 21572481; e-mail: h3240@accor-hotels.com. Busy hotel in the middle of the tourist area, buffet style menu. Underwaterworld Dive Centre is located on the premises. **Crowne Plaza**, Tigne St, Sliema, SLM 11; tel (356) 21341173/fax (356) 21311292; e-mail: hotel@crowneplazamalta.com. Large and impersonal with three restaurants, two pools, facilities for disabled. **Grand Hotel Mercure Selmun Palace**, Selmun, Mellieha SPB 10; tel (356) 21521040/fax (356) 21521060. Close to Cirkewwa and Anchor Bay. Buffet-style food, two pools, facilities for disabled. **Mellieha Bay Hotel**, Ghadira, Mellieha, SPB 10; tel

(356) 21573844/fax (356) 21576399. Next to the beach, three pools, lido, with Aquaventure Diving and Watersports resort. **Ramla Bay Complex**, Ramla Bay, Marfa SPB 10; tel (356) 21573521/fax (356) 21575931; e-mail: ramlabay@digigate.net. On the north side, ideal for the ferry and all northern diving. With its own dive centre (look for the converted blue fire truck). Private beach, pool, facilities for disabled. **Victoria Hotel**, Gorg Borg Olivier St, Sliema, SM12; tel (356) 21334711/fax (356) 21334771; www.victoriahotel.com. Excellent four star hotel with a roof top pool, in the heart of Sliema fairly close to Dive Systems. **Suncrest Hotel**, Qawra Coast Rd, Qawra SPB 08; tel (356) 21577101/fax (356) 21581166; e-mail: info@suncresthotels.com. Huge hotel, large rooms with sea views; restaurant open round the clock, lido, own dive centre (seasonal). **Westin Dragonara Resort**, Dragonara Complex, St Julian's Bay STJ 02; tel (356) 21377884/fax (356) 21378877. International style, two pools, health club, facilities for disabled, with Divewise Services.

WHERE TO EAT

The hotels listed above all have good restaurants and there are around 700 other licensed restaurants on Malta to choose from.

Barracuda, Main St, St Julian's; tel (356) 21331817. Formal dining, superb service, but comparatively expensive. **Il Brigante**, Ball St, Paceville, Sliema; tel (356) 21311774. Excellent value, Maltese specialities and half-price menus for children. **Coral Reef**, opposite Suncrest Hotel, Qawra; tel (356) 21577101. Moderately priced, superb pasta and seafood dishes. **Marina Seafood Restaurant**, Xatt is-Sajjieda, Marsaxlokk; tel (356) 21871202. Great value, busy for the catch of the day. **Mullins**, Church St, St Paul's Bay; tel (356) 21583473. Great spaghetti and seafood, reasonably priced, though does get busy. **Rebekah's**, Triq lt-Tgham, Mellieha; tel (356) 21521145. Family-owned converted farmhouse, warm and friendly (no children under 13 allowed). **Royal Overseas Café**, St Lucia St, Valletta; tel (356) 21248632. Excellent pizzeria, sandwiches, a local favourite. **Trattoria**, Tunny Net Complex, Marfa Rd, Mellieha Bay; tel (356) 21521331/fax (356) 21521233. Excellent Italian food, fish, steaks and pasta. **Trattoria Palazz**, 43 Old Theatre St, Valletta; tel (356) 21226611. Wonderful Italian-style pastas, good service, reasonable prices and spotlessly clean. **The Winston**, High St, Sliema; tel (356) 21335800. Fish specialities, pasta and local dishes, outdoor dining in the summer.

DIVE FACILITIES

There are over 40 registered diving operations on Malta. A complete list is available from branches of the Maltese Tourist Office overseas (see page 16), or from the Federation of Underwater Activities

in Malta (FUAM), PO Box 29, Gzira, Malta. **Abyss Diving Club**, Dolmen Resort Hotel, Qawra, St. Paul's, SPB05; tel (356) 21581510; e-mail info@abyssdivingclub.com. **Anchor Dive Systems**, Triq il-Lampuki Street, St. Paul's , SPB03; tel (356) 79267817 / 99449697; e-mail info@anchordiving.com. **Aqua Bubbles Dive School**, Corinthia Jerma Palace Hotel, Dawret it-Torri, Marsaskala, ZBR10; tel (356) 21639292/ 21633222 ext.1155; e-mail info@aquabubbles.co.uk. **Aquanauts Dive School**, 60, Xatt Ta' Tigne, Sliema, SLM02; www.maltascuba.com. **Aquarrigo Scuba Diving Centre**, Preluna Beach Club, Triq it-Tori, Sliema, SLM01; tel (356) 21330882/fax (356) 21380699; e-mail info@planetsea.net. **Aquatica Diving & Fishing Centre**, 54, Triq Toni Bajada, St. Paul's, SPB02; tel/fax (356) 21579753; mobile 79493122; www.aquaticamalta.com. **Aquaventure Ltd.**, Mellieha Bay Hotel, Ghadira Bay, Mellieha, MLH02; tel (356) 21522141/fax (356) 21521053; e-mail info@aquaventuremalta.com. **Aquaworld Diving Centre,** Sliema Aquatic Sports Club, Triq it-Torri, Sliema, SLM01; tel (356) 21318893; e-mail info@maltadiving.net. **Buddies Dive Cove**, 24/2 Pioneer Road, Bugibba, SPB03; tel/fax (356) 21576266; www.buddiesmalta.com. **Cresta Diving Quay**, Cresta Quay Beach Club, St.George's Bay, St. Julian's, STJ02; tel (356) 21310743/ fax (356) 21372589; e-mail info@ crestadiving.com. **Dawn Divers**, Ramla Bay Resort, Ramla Bay, Mellieha, MLH02; tel (356) 21522181/fax (356) 21575931; e-mail info@dawndiversmalta.com. **Dive Care**, St. George's Bay, St. Julians, STJ02; tel (356) 21319994/fax (356) 21341729; e-mail divecare@digigate.net. **Dive Deep Blue**, 100, Triq Ananija, Bugibba, SPB06; tel (356) 21583946/fax (356) 21583945; e-mail dive@divedeepblue.com. **Dive Med Diving Centre**, Ponta taz-Zonqor, Marsaskala, ZBR09; tel/fax (356) 21639981; e-mail info@divemed.com. **Dive Shack,** 14a Qui si sana Place, Sliema, SLM11; tel (356) 21338558/fax (356) 21345670; e-mail info@diveshackscuba.com. **Dive Systems Ltd,** Tower Point, Tower Road, Exiles, Sliema, SLM09; tel (356) 21319123/fax (356) 21342040; e-mail info@divesystemsmalta.com. **Divewise Services Ltd,** Westin Dragonara Resort, Dragonara Road, St Julians, STJ02; tel (356)21356 441/fax (356) 21310708; e-mail info@divewise.com.mt. **Maltaqua Ltd,** Triton Court, Mosta Road, St Paul's Bay, SPB03; tel (356) 21571873/fax (356) 21580064; e-mail info@maltaqua.com. **Meldives Dive School,** Tunny Net Lido Complex, Marfa Road, Mellieha Bay, MLH02; tel/fax (356) 21522595; e-mail meldives@ digigate.net. **Neptune Dives,** Main Street, Balluta, St Julian's, STJ01; tel (356) 9982046; e-mail info@neptunesdives.com. **Northeast Diving Services Ltd,** 9, Belvedere Street, Gzira, GZR05; tel (356) 21340511/fax (356) 21340511; e-mail dereknds@onvol.net. **Octopus Garden Diving Centre,** Gilleru Harbour Hotel, Church Square, St Paul's,

SPB05; tel/fax (356) 21578725. **Sol Suncrest Hotel**, Qawra Coast Road, Qawra Salina Bay, tel/fax (356) 21584318; www.octopus-garden.com. **Paradise Diving and Watersports**, Paradise Bay Hotel, Cirkewwa, Mellieha, MLH02; tel (356) 21574116/fax (356) 21524366; e-mail alison@paradisediving.com. **Scubatech**, Triq il-Alka, St Paul's Bay, SPB03; tel (356) 21455916/fax (356) 21580617; e-mail dive@scubatech.info. **Seashell Dive Cove**, Pergola Club Hotel, 2B, Triq Dun Frangisk, Sciberras, Mellieha, MLH06; tel/fax (356) 21521062; e-mail seashell@vol.net.mt. **Sharks, British Sub Aqua Club No.1818**, meet at Maltaqua, Mosta Road, St Paul's Bay every Saturday at 13.30; tel Jules Christians (356) 21314055; e-mail jules@melita.net. **Starfish Diving School**, Corinthia Beach Club, St George's Bay, St Julian's, STJ02; tel (356) 21382995/fax (356) 21382915; e-mail info@starfishdiving.com. **Strand Diving Services**, Ramon Perellos St, St Paul's Bay, SPB02; tel (356) 21574502/fax (356) 21577480; e-mail strand@ waldonet.net.mt. **Subway**, Pioneer Road, Bugibba, SPB03; tel (356) 21570354/ fax (356) 21577086; c/o Barcelo Riviera Resort & Spa, Marfa Bay, SPB10; tel (356) 21572997/fax (356) 21577086; www.subwayscuba.com. **Underwaterworld**, Grand Hotel Mercure San Antonio, Tourist St, Bugibba, SPB04; tel (356) 21503643/4 / 21584422; e-mail underwaterworld@onvol.net; www.lunadiving.com.

FILM PROCESSING

Foto Vision, 10 Old Treasury St, Valletta VLT 04; tel (356) 21221610/fax (356) 21236190. Also at: 87 Paola Square, Paola PLA 04, tel (356) 21672079; 84 Valley Rd, B'Kara BKR 10, tel (356) 21993529. Does E6 processing.**The Foto Grapher**, St Thomas St, Fgura PLA 14; tel (356) 21661380/fax (356) 21809474. Does E6 processing.

EMERGENCIES

There are pharmacies all over Malta. In a medical emergency, there is a helicopter service with a direct link to the nearest hospital and hyperbaric chamber. All decompression accidents are taken this way.

Emergency	tel 196
Fire	tel 199
Police	tel 191
Hyperbaric Unit	tel (356) 21234766
St Luke's Hospital	tel (356) 21241251,
	(356) 21247860

LOCAL HIGHLIGHTS

Malta's capital, **Valletta**, located between two huge harbours and surrounded by massive fortifications, is not to be missed. The city is laid out in a grid pattern, with eight main streets criss-crossed by numerous narrow, stepped side streets. Sights include the magnificent Palace of the Grand Masters, St John's Co-Cathedral with its sumptuous interior, and several museums.

Among the island's many **ancient neolithic sites** are the temples at Tarxien. Believed to date from between 3000 and 2500BC, they are remarkable for the quality of their stone carving. Access is from Valletta Bus Terminus, buses 11 and 26 (stop near Tarxien police station).

Mdina, set within massive walls further protected by an enclosed dry moat, was established by the Romans on a Bronze Age site. Covering only 4ha (10 acres), the walled city is largely pedestrianized (apart

KARROZINI

Karrozini are traditional horse-drawn carriages, which can be found in *karrozini* ranks at Sliema, St Julian's, Valletta and outside the gateway at Mdina. These carriages have been plying their trade here since the 1850s and some are over one hundred years old. *Karrozini* offer a great way to tour the sights, but always agree on a fare before starting out (*karrozin* drivers are hardened bargainers).

from the *karrozini*) and is perfect for exploring on foot. There are viewing points around the walls. Sights include the Baroque cathedral, palaces, churches, museums, a convent, small piazzas and some splendid houses belonging to the Maltese aristocracy.

An organized jeep safari of the island is an interesting possibility, with pick-up from your hotel, or you can take a helicopter sightseeing tour around the islands. Trips are organized by **Captain Morgan's**, Dolphin Court, Tigné Seafront, Sliema; tel (356) 21343373/fax (356) 21332004/e-mail: info@captainmorgan.com.mt.

A locally produced monthly *What's On* magazine is available in hotels and shops.

TOURIST INFORMATION

Tourist Information Centre: 1 City Gate, Valletta; tel (356) 21237747.

The Marfa Ridge is the location of many of the island's most popular dive sites.

In Roman mythology Neptune's chariot was drawn by white seahorses. These beautiful creatures are among the most fascinating fish to be found in the Mediterranean. Members of the family Sygnathidae, which also includes pipefish and sea dragons, they belong to the subgroup Hippocampus (from the Greek *hippos*, horse, and *kampe*, worm or caterpillar).

Around 35 true species of seahorse have been described around the world, although there have been many more wrongly identified members of the family thanks to the seahorse's chameleon-like ability to change colour. In European waters two species are to be found: the short-snouted seahorse (*Hippocampus*

hippocampus) and the maned seahorse (*Hippocampus ramulosus*). The latter is the one more commonly found in Maltese waters and is known locally as *Ziemel tal-bahar*.

PHYSICAL CHARACTERISTICS

Their general form is well engraved in popular imagination, with a horse-shaped head set at an angle to the body, the trunk of which is generally short and fat, and tapering to a long, prehensile tail. The snout is long and straight, while body rings carry bony tubercles, giving the seahorse an almost angular and knobbly appearance. The top and back of the head and body are covered in

fleshy strands, like the mane of a horse, often with bits of algae and detritus attached, further enhancing its camouflage techniques. Seahorses can change their body colour to match their surrounds (generally the algae turf that grows all around the islands).

MALE PREGNANCY

The seahorses found around the Maltese archipelago grow to maximum of 15cm (6in) in length and are usually found in their lifelong mating pairs. They have a complex mating ritual which may last for several days, involving ceremonial greetings and intricate dances, after which the female transfers her eggs by means of an ovipositor (inverted oviduct) into a specially adapted 'brood pouch' located in front of the male's abdomen. It is here that the eggs are fertilized and where they develop, oxygenated by tiny capillaries that line the pouch. Further bathed in placental fluid, the eggs hatch inside the pouch and, after a short 'pregnancy', the male lowers the temperature in the pouch to that of the surrounding water, gradually expelling the live and swimming brood. Adult seahorses take no further interest in their offspring, which are able immediately to fend for themselves. They feed on small shrimp and other tiny planktonic crustacea, picking at

Opposite: *Seahorses like this Hippocampus ramulosus are a rare and delightful find.*
Above: *Well camouflaged, seahorses often have bits of algae attached to their bony tubercules.*

them with their long snouts and sucking them up into their mouths like vacuum cleaners.

Unfortunately they are not adept at swimming, having only one dorsal fin for propulsion and very small ear-like pectoral fins for steering and stabilization in the water, while their prehensile tail wraps around a suitable piece of algae when they are at a rest. There are no anal or tail fins.

Seahorses are most often found in shallow brackish water such as at the entrance to the Ghasri Valley and even in Valletta harbour. With only a few natural enemies, such as crabs and other fish, their greatest danger is from humans, who have developed an unhealthy interest in the animals because of their curiosity value. Chinese herbal medicine also uses dried seahorses to treat ailments ranging from asthma and arthritis to impotence and incontinence.

Endowed with beauty and mystique, seahorses have been a source of inspiration since time immemorial. Now that their survival is at stake, the pleasure of finding one must be accompanied by awareness.

COMINO

Originally known as Kemmuna, after a type of cumin spice plant that once grew here, the island of Comino is situated mid-channel between Malta and Gozo and is only 2.7 sq km (1 sq mile) in area. The ferry from either Cirkewwa on Malta or Mgarr on Gozo drops you off at the landing stage at the Comino Hotel. From here a number of nature trails traverse the island.

Although generally barren in appearance, the island offers spectacular views from its southwestern cliffs across towards Malta. Once a haven for pirates, Comino is dominated by a square tower built in 1618 by Grand Master Alof de Wignacourt to protect the Comino Channel against raiders. The island is now a designated National Park and is home to several interesting plants and nesting birds, including owls and bats (which are protected).

Comino has become a major centre for divers, snorkellers and boat-trippers. Pleasure craft make a daily pilgrimage to the legendary Blue Lagoon, a sheltered, shallow lagoon nestling between the main island of Comino and its smaller sister islet of Cominotto. For divers, the northern shore is indented by numerous caves and caverns, many of which can be accessed on the surface as well as underwater. All are teeming with fish, principally chromis, sand smelt and saddled bream, partly on account of the popularity of this area with snorkellers for fish feeding.

To the southwest of the island, a small lighthouse tower on the point marks the location of the spectacular Lighthouse Reef (Site 13). The reef here drops vertically to a huge tumble of boulders and a superb chimney that dissects the cliff. This is without doubt the best site on the small island and most dive centres organize boat trips here from either Malta or Gozo. Note that Comino does have its own dive centre and arrangements can be made in advance to link a ferry trip to the island to catch the dive boat and return in plenty of time.

Opposite: *Charter boats visit the legendary Blue Lagoon every day.*
Above: *The painted comber, a small member of the seabass family, is relatively tame.*

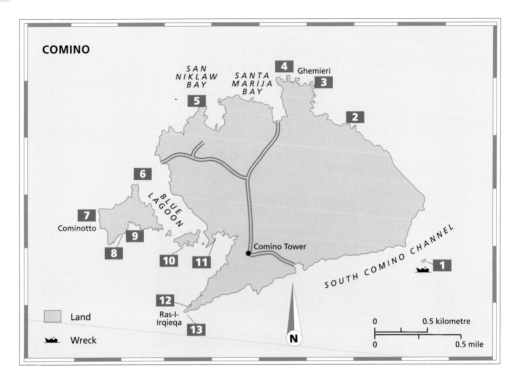

COMINO

SAN NIKLAW BAY

SANTA MARIJA BAY

4 Ghemieri

3

5

2

6

BLUE LAGOON

7

Cominotto

9

8

10　**11**

Comino Tower

12

Ras-l-Irqieqa

13

SOUTH COMINO CHANNEL

1

Land

Wreck

N

0　　0.5 kilometre

0　　0.5 mile

1 SULTAN ROCK
★★★

Location: Off the southeastern point of Comino, on the Malta side of the island.

Access: By boat.

Conditions: Fairly sheltered from the northeasterly winds, but can be choppy with strong current at times.

Average depth: 6m (20ft)

Maximum depth: 18m (60ft)

Average visibility: 30m (100ft)

This dive is for more experienced divers as current is to be expected. Although the dive is not especially deep, there is a danger of being swept off, particularly in open water. The dive takes place over and around huge boulders covered in all sorts of algae, including sea cactus (*Halimeda tuna*) and peacock's tail (*Padina pavonica*). There are small patches of *Posidonia*, where several species of wrasse are always to be found. Moray eels are present, as are amberjacks (*Seriola dumerili*), an abundance of painted comber (*Serranus scriba*), and grouper (*Epinephelus guaza*). You can also see the remnants of HMS *Sultan*, an 18th-century battleship which has mostly been salvaged, although a few bits and pieces remain.

2 SANTA MARIJA TUNNEL (ELEPHANT ROCK)
★★★★★

Location: Inside the sheltered headland, the northeastern part of Comino.

Access: By boat.

Conditions: Sheltered from the southwest winds and therefore very popular with snorkellers.

Average depth: 6m (20ft)

Maximum depth: 6m (20ft)

Average visibility: 15m (50ft)

This tunnel runs about 30m (100ft) through the headland and is a fairly easy dive. Divers and snorkellers

---

SPONGES [*SPONZA*]

The yellow sponge (*Clathrina clathrus*) and the pink sponge (*Oscarella lobularis*) are two common species found on the deeper reefs off the wall and in caverns. You will also find columnar sponges (*Axinella cannabina* and *Axinella polypoides*) in similar habitats, but perhaps the most common of all is the Greek bathing sponge (*Spongia officinalis*), which has been fished for centuries. Once removed from its rocky substrate, the sponge is strung through with a sturdy rope and suspended in a current-swept area until the animal is dead, leaving the spongy interior.

are recommended to carry lights to pick out the brilliant colours of the sponges, bryozoans and golden cup corals that line the walls. There are few fish in the cave except around the entrances, where large schools of chromis and bream congregate.

3 SANTA MARIJA CAVES

★★★★★★★

Location: Northwest of Santa Marija Tunnel (Site 2) to the large natural arch.
Access: By boat.
Conditions: Sheltered from the northwest winds and very popular with fish-feeding tourists.
Average depth: 7m (24ft)
Maximum depth: 10m (33ft)
Average visibility: 18m (60ft)
This is a large cave and cavern system which extends over 30m (100ft) all the way through the headland and connects to another cave. At the junction there is a shaft open to the sky, which considerably increases the pleasure of the dive. Santa Marija is a popular site for fish feeding; whether you are in favour of or against the practice, there are certainly thousands of fish in the area and most tourists enjoy the encounter. If you do feed the fish, always remember to take out the plastic bags from the water afterwards. Fish species include saddled bream (*Oblada melanura*), two-banded bream (*Diplodus vulgaris*) and chromis.

4 SANTA MARIJA REEF

★★★★★★

Location: Opposite the northernmost point of Comino.
Access: By boat.
Conditions: Some current to be expected. Generally good visibility as the seabed is gravel.
Average depth: 9m (30ft)
Maximum depth: 21m (70ft)
Average visibility: 25m (80ft)
The dive boat anchors in 9m (30ft), from where you can start to explore the numerous gulleys, caverns, swimthroughs and caves. This site is excellent for photography as there are lots of opportunities for wide-angle cave shots. It is a low rocky reef heavily covered in algae and is a good place to spot grouper, mullet and most of the bream species, including large schools of salema (*Sarpa salpa*). These fish reach quite a size and form large schools that graze on the algae.

> ### TUBE WORMS [*HANEX TAL-WARDA*]
>
> There are a number of segmented worms that live in tubes around the Maltese islands. All are light- and pressure-sensitive, preferring recesses under large boulders or inside caves and caverns. The most common is the featherduster worm (*Bispira voluticornis*). Similarly sized though different in colour is the white-tufted worm (*Protula tubularia*), found in small clumps on walls. The largest of the tube worms is the magnificent peacock worm (*Sabella pavonina*), a solitary animal in shallow waters though often seen in numbers attached to deeper wrecks. This tube worm is common on muddy substrates and can be found all through the Mediterranean and as far north as Scandinavia. When taking photographs of tube worms, use a longer-focusing lens so as not to disturb them. You may get only one chance as the light from your flash will cause the worm to react by retreating rapidly back into its protective tube.

5 THE CANYON

★★★★

Location: Off the headland directly out to the left of the Comino Hotel.
Access: By boat, but can be reached from the shore.
Conditions: Sheltered between the two sides of rock, but there can be surge all the way through.
Average depth: 7m (24ft)
Maximum depth: 20m (66ft)
Average visibility: 21m (70ft)
The canyon has near-vertical sides and many small mini-drop-offs and narrow tunnels created by the rock formations. The remains of a small Maltese fishing boat have become lodged in some rocks, but they are rapidly deteriorating. Fish life is not very prolific and the rocks are covered in algal fuzz. Popular as a night dive, the canyon is home to many different species of starfish, nudibranchs and small crabs.

6 BLUE LAGOON

★★★

Location: To the north of the sheltered Blue Lagoon.
Access: By boat, but can be snorkelled from the shore.
Conditions: Sheltered from the worst of storms and very popular with tourists.
Average depth: 6m (20ft)
Maximum depth: 12m (40ft)
Average visibility: 25m (80ft)
This site is very popular with swimmers and snorkellers but has little to offer. Always very busy with tourists and boat traffic, there are usually large schools of salema (*Sarpa salpa*) and plenty of chromis. The bottom of the

---

GROUPER/SEABASS [CERNA]

A few species of grouper and seabass are found around these islands, with the most common grouper being *Epinephelus guaza* [*Cerna gigas*], which can grow up to 1m (3ft). The most common of the smaller related species is the painted comber (*Serranus scriba*) [*Burqax*]. This delightful fish can grow up to 35cm (14in) and is mainly found amidst algae on walls, reefs and wrecks. Unfortunately, grouper are a favourite quarry of illegal spearfishermen, who have hunted them out of the shallow rocky reefs and chased them into deeper waters, making them particularly timid.

---

lagoon changes from sand to *Posidonia* and there are always large numbers of wrasse. Seahorses have also been seen in this location.

7 OUTER COMINOTTO REEF
★★★

Location: Northwest of Cominotto island to the edge of the outer reef drop-off.
Access: By boat.
Conditions: An exposed site, subject to surge, swell and current.
Average depth: 18m (60ft)
Maximum depth: 36m (120ft)
Average visibility: 30m (100ft)
This is a wall dive mainly created by massive boulders, which, underneath, have interesting holes and caverns where shade-loving creatures such as burrowing anemones (*Cerianthus membranaceus*) and peacock worms (*Sabella pavonina*) hide. The site's name comes from the numerous anchors that have been snagged amidst the boulder reef and drop-off. You can expect to find dentex, chromis, bream and small patches of *Posidonia*, where you may also be lucky enough to find broad-mouth pipefish (*Sygnathus typhle*).

8 COMINOTTO ANCHOR REEF
★★★★

Location: Off the south coast of Cominotto.
Access: By boat.
Conditions: Exposed, with current to be expected, and therefore only for experienced divers.
Average depth: 12m (40ft)
Maximum depth: 50m (165ft)
Average visibility: 30m (100ft)
This is a vertical wall with little large fish life apart from huge numbers of chromis. The wall drops to 39m (127ft) and some very big boulders, which have created swimthroughs and caverns where brightly

coloured sponges and golden cup corals can be found. You can also find grouper in these deeper sections. On the way down, you should be able to see an old four-pointed anchor.

9 INNER COMINOTTO
★★★★★

Location: Off the southern shore of Cominotto.
Access: By boat.
Conditions: Fairly sheltered from the northeast winds, but can have surge and choppy surface waters.
Average depth: 9m (30ft)
Maximum depth: 22m (73ft)
Average visibility: 25m (80ft)
The dive boat tends to anchor near the corner of the headland close to a lovely natural arch in the limestone island. From this point divers can take either the route to the left or the route to the right; the site is often covered as two separate dives. There are large rocks all topped with algae and patches of *Posidonia*. The bottom of the wall has a number of small caves where cardinalfish (*Apogon imberbis*) and brilliantly coloured starfish can be found. There is a pleasing overhang at 7m (24ft) and you can swim from here through the arch and back to the dive boat.

10 COMINOTTO CAVE (ALEX'S CAVE)
★★★★

Location: Although known as Cominotto Cave, this dive is to the south of the next large islet between Cominotto and Comino. Behind this islet is the Blue Lagoon.
Access: By boat.
Conditions: Quite sheltered, except when a southerly storm blows the tidal surge into the cave; at such times it is extremely dangerous and should be avoided.
Average depth: 8m (27ft)
Maximum depth: 16m (53ft)
Average visibility: 15m (50ft)
A popular second dive after Inner Lantern Point (Site 12), this is an interesting cave carved out by wave action, with a sandy bottom and smooth sides. Algae debris tends to collect on the floor of the cave. On entering, you swim 15m (50ft) into the gloomy recess, so a torch is recommended. There is a chimney at the back of the cave and you can surface to natural light, but only when the sea is flat calm. From here, divers can return to the boat, or continue on to the Crystal Lagoon (Site 11) through the tunnel in the next headland, but most divers do not have enough air for this length of dive. There are lots of *Posidonia*, though very few fish, and the caves are the highlight of the dive.

Above: *Small tube worms retreat quickly into their hole if divers get too close.*
Below: *Polycirrus spread their sticky tentacles over rocks to catch planktonic and algal debris.*

Large banks or meadows of Posidonia oceanica are found almost everywhere.

11 CRYSTAL LAGOON
★★★

Location: Inside the sheltered inlet at Crystal Lagoon on the southwest of Comino.
Access: By boat, but can also be reached from the small jetty.
Conditions: Sheltered from the northwest winds and therefore very popular with snorkellers.
Average depth: 12m (40ft)
Maximum depth: 15m (50ft)
Average visibility: 15m (50ft)
The dive follows the tunnel that cuts through the headland to the west of the island. The bottom of the cave is littered with boulders and is therefore generally clear of silt. There are few fish in the area until you come back into the sheltered lagoon, where saddled bream and two-bar bream, used to being hand-fed, hover around the dive boat in expectation of a free meal. The seabed is covered in *Posidonia* grass, and it was here that we found our first cuttlefish (*Sepia officinalis*).

12 INNER LANTERN POINT
★★★★★★

Location: Inside the headland to the north of the light on the southwest point of Comino.
Access: By boat.
Conditions: Sheltered from the southeast winds, but surge and current are to be expected.
Average depth: 30m (100ft)
Maximum depth: Beyond 45m (150ft)
Average visibility: Beyond 30m (100ft)
Popular with most of the dive operators who come by boat from Malta, this is a dramatic dive down a vertical wall, which tumbles into huge boulders interspersed with large patches of *Posidonia*. As you work along the wall (keeping it to your right) you come to a vertical slash in the limestone, with a shallow cave. The floor of the cave has large peacock worms (*Sabella pavonina*) and burrowing anemones (*Cerianthus membranaceus*). Cardinalfish, bream and millions of chromis abound, but there are no big fish.

13 L-IRQIEQA (LANTERN POINT) (LIGHTHOUSE REEF)
★★★★★

Location: On the southern (more exposed) side of the light on the southwest point of Comino.
Access: By boat.
Conditions: Exposed and generally difficult unless the weather is perfect.
Average depth: 18m (60ft)
Maximum depth: Beyond 50m (165ft)
Average visibility: Beyond 30m (100ft)
This is a spectacular dive down from a low rocky shelf at 6m (20ft), where the dive boat anchors. You start the dive at the entrance to a chimney, which drops down and through the limestone plateau and exits at 16m (54ft). The tunnel is wide enough for divers to manoeuvre without touching the sides. Here you will find white-tufted worms (*Protula tubularia*) and lots of fireworms (*Hermodice carunculata*). The gravel base at the mouth of the cavern has a small group of purple heart urchins (*Spatangus purpureus*). Spiny starfish (*Marthasterias glacialis*) are common on the massive outer boulders that drop down into the depths. These boulders have also created huge caverns and swimthroughs. This is the best dive around the island.

HOW TO GET THERE

By ferry: This is a popular route, with eight trips daily from both Cirkewwa on Malta and Mgarr harbour on Gozo. The Comino Hotel owns the ferry, so additional pick-ups can be arranged to suit. The return ticket costs Lm 2 and is free to all visitors residing on the island. Booking is not necessary, but residents and employees of the hotel are given priority when the boat is full.

By boat: Many sightseeing boat trips also make the daily pilgrimage to Comino to visit the sheltered and shallow Blue Lagoon. Trips can be booked in advance from any of the hotels on Malta or Gozo.

GETTING AROUND

There are no cars or roads on Comino; a track links the Comino Hotel with its sister bungalows on the island.

WHERE TO STAY AND EAT

Comino Hotel, Comino
tel (356) 21529821–9/fax (356) 21529826

Sales: tel (356) 21233636–7/
fax (356) 21239057
An exclusive hotel built in the early 1960s. 150 rooms and a further separate 45 self-catering bungalows located elsewhere on the island in their own sheltered bay. The buffet-style meals are superb. Sports facilities include several swimming pools and tennis courts with instruction.

DIVE FACILITIES

Tony's Dive Services, Subway Scuba Diving Centre, Comino Hotel, Comino
tel (356) 21580611/fax (356) 21573654;
e-mail: subway@maltanet.net
There is a good-sized boat for divers, and the owner has in-depth knowlege of local reefs. The dive centre is open only from Easter to November, but dive trips can be made during the winter months by arrangement.

EMERGENCIES

In a medical emergency, there is a helicopter pad with direct links to the nearest hospital and hyperbaric chamber on Malta. All decompression accidents are ferried this way.

Emergency	tel 112
Hyperbaric Unit	tel (356) 21234766
Gozo General	tel (356) 21561600,
Hospital	(356) 21556851
St Luke's Hospital,	tel (356) 21241251,
Malta	(356) 21247860

LOCAL HIGHLIGHTS

Comino is a small island and a designated national park. There are excellent scenic walks to the **Comino Tower** in the centre of the island as well as to the **Crystal Lagoon**, **Santa Marija Bay** with its little church and square, and the legendary Blue Lagoon.

The **Blue Lagoon** is a narrow channel separating Comino from Cominotto, where the shallow bay and its white sandy bottom reflect upwards beautiful shades of blue. This marvellous spot attracts many day-trippers.

All watersports are catered for at the Comino Hotel, including canoeing, jetskiing, windsurfing, sailing and snorkelling.

Day-trippers relax in the shallow, warm waters of the marvellous Blue Lagoon.

Night diving has been classed as an adventure within an adventure. Popular night dives around the islands are at Cirkewwa Point (Malta, Site 27), the Blue Hole, Xlendi Cave and Reef, Mgarr ix-Xini (Gozo, sites 12, 18, 24), and the Canyon (Comino, Site 5). Once you have chosen your night-dive location, it is advisable if possible to familiarize yourself with the site by diving the area during the day. Then one of the easiest ways of introducing yourself to night diving is to dive at dusk and acclimatize yourself slowly to the change between ambient light and the artificial light of your dive lights.

No special training is required, but divers and underwater photographers should be even more aware at night of their buoyancy control to avoid damaging delicate cup corals and crustose algae. If you must steady yourself and touch the coral, always choose an area of dead coral rock and only use one finger to steady yourself.

Night-Diving Tips
- Attend a night-diving instruction course.
- Dive with someone who is acquainted not only with the dive site but with night conditions.
- Carry one or two spare torches.
- When entering the water, take a compass bearing to the shore or nearest mooring buoy.
- Inform someone at your hotel or dive shop of your dive plan and your estimated time of exit from the water.
- Have warm dry clothing ready to change into after the dive.

Photography at Night

A flash is a prerequisite for photography at night. Few flash units have the power output or angle of coverage for extreme wide-angle applications, so a close-up or macro lens is most commonly used. Coupled with a slow film such as Fuji Velvia, the result can be beautifully rich colours with seemingly no water between you and the subject. The rule for choosing film is that the slower the speed of film, the higher the colour saturation will be.

The most striking aspect of diving at night is that the true colours of the reef are shown in all their vibrancy, illuminated by the light of your torches and flash. During the day, due to the refraction and absorption of light by water, the colour red is lost by a depth of only 2m (6ft).

Night-time is also the best time to take marine life-study photographs, as many species on the reef sleep at night and can be approached more easily then. Be especially sensitive, however, when approaching sleeping creatures. Although it may be tempting to fire off lots of film on a particularly photogenic subject, never cause sleeping patterns to be disrupted. Creeping up on a snoozing parrotfish can induce fear and flight, causing it to blunder about the reef, breaking corals and damaging itself. Instead, line up your shot on a piece of coral nearby and then move quickly into position, taking a couple of photographs as a maximum of each subject before turning your lights away. Delicate marine creatures such as seahorses should be photographed only about three times, and then left alone. Never interfere with active night hunters and foragers such as moray eels.

You may get only one chance to photograph many of the smaller fan worms, for instance, because of the intensity of the flash's light output. Most nocturnal creatures are sensitive to both light and pressure, so approach them patiently and sympathetically. Strength of flash output is variable depending on manufacturer's specifications, but the best choice of all to avoid causing distress is to use a flash with full TTL (through-the-lens) capabilities. This allows the flash to do the thinking for you. Remember that night diving is in itself difficult to do, so the easier you can make the steps of your photography the better.

Illuminating the subject prior to exposure is critical and a sensible type of flash to use is one fitted with an internal

modelling light (independently powered so as not to drain power from the flash output). The one I personally recommend is the YS300 made by Sea & Sea. Alternatively, you can strap a slimline torch to the exterior of another type of flash so as to free your hands to operate the camera controls. A red spot light is perfect as it will not interfere with your night vision and is less obtrusive to marine life.

The nudibranch Hypselodoris valenciennesi is often seen during night dives.

NIGHTLIFE ON THE REEF

Colourful cowrie shells and other molluscs such as nudibranchs or sea slugs actively browse at night amongst the algae that grow on dead corals. Creatures that have been hiding in nooks and crannies or under boulders to avoid the glare of the midday sun now crawl, slither and hop into the open. Hermit crabs joust with each other over possession of empty mollusc shells and sea urchins, and featherstars crawl onto the reeftop.

Animals difficult to photograph during the day, such as the peacock worm (*Sabella pavonina*), can be confronted more readily. Small blennies and shrimps now dare you to come closer, while the banded shrimp (*Stenopus spinosus*) and white-spotted octopus (*Octopus macropus*) can be easily approached as they wander over the algae turf that covers most of the rocky shoreline. Scorpionfish also appear much more brightly coloured at night.

In your search for interesting fish or invertebrates, do not overlook the design or delicate formation of stationary corals such as the golden zoanthid (*Parazoanthus axinellae*) or other individual coral polyps and algae. By the light from your torches you can start to pick out all the colours you missed during the day, as well as observing and photographing creatures that lie hidden deep within the reef crevices or under the sandy seabed during daylight hours. Night diving is truly spectacular and every dive is bound to be different.

GOZO

The smaller of the two main Maltese islands, Gozo, lies 8km (5 miles) to the northwest of Malta. The island is 15km (9¹/₂ miles) long by 7km (4¹/₂ miles) at its widest point, with a total of 43km (27 miles) of coastline. Like its big sister, Gozo features an impressive inland citadel at Victoria (Rabat); nearly all the main roads radiate from this city.

Although distinguished by a layer of blue-clay soil, Gozo shares some geological characteristics with Malta. Much of the island slopes gently into the sea before it plunges into the depths, while on the west and south coasts towering cliffs plummet an equal distance underwater, making the diving experience spectacular. Indeed the diving is even more scenic than on Malta, with dramatic vertical cliff faces, natural arches and caves – Gozo is unquestionably one of the most popular diving destinations in the Mediterranean. For convenience we have divided the island into three areas.

As in all island locations, the diving is dependent on the weather. Several of the more popular sheltered sites are prone to rainwater run-off, which can reduce the underwater visibility to nil because of the suspended particulate washed down from the limestone hills, though this rarely lasts for long. The **north** shore from Marsalforn to the Ghasri Valley has deep water directly off the limestone shore, so visibility here is generally good.

By far the best diving in the archipelago is in the **southwest** at Dwejra Point. Here, divers can visit two natural wonders of the Mediterranean: the gigantic arch known as the Azure Window (Site 11) at the tip of Dwejra Point, and inland from this rocky outcrop the Inland Sea (Site 10), a sheltered lagoon cut by an awesome fissure which runs through the headland, offering divers 25m (80ft) of depth below underhanging cliffs. Further to the south, the landmass rears up vertically, with few entry points except at Xlendi Bay.

From St Andrew's Divers Cove towards the **east** of the island much of the coastline is accessed by boat. In particular, dive boat is the only way to reach the caves below the awesome ramparts of the Ta' Cenc Cliffs.

Opposite: *The Azure Window is a distinctive landmark at Dwejra Point.*
Above: *Small nooks and crannies frequently have cardinalfish (Apogon imberbis) in residence.*

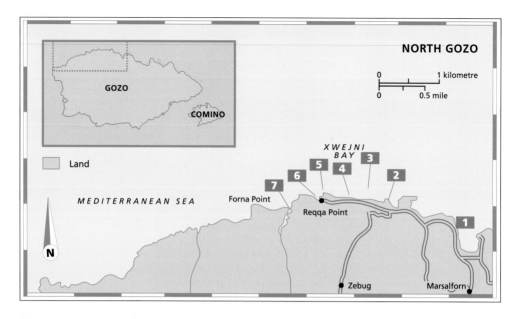

1 MARSALFORN BAY

★★★

Location: Off the breakwater to the northwest of Marsalforn Bay.
Access: From the shore.
Conditions: Generally sheltered; normally used as a beginner's dive.
Average depth: 8m (27ft)
Maximum depth: 12m (40ft)
Average visibility: 15m (50ft)

ANEMONES [ARTIKLA]

A relative of jellyfish, corals and stinging hydroids, anemones come in many different shapes and sizes. The snakelocks anemone (Anemonia viridis) has long tentacles tipped with a purple or green knob; the tentacles are armed with stinging cells called nematocysts with which the anemone paralyses its prey. Small shrimps and crabs are always found in association with the snakelocks anemone. The golden anemone (Condylactis aurantiaca) is more commonly found on the sandy seabed, with most of its body hidden from sight. There are large numbers of this anemone to be found all around the wreck of the Rozi at Marfa Point on Malta (Site 26). The burrowing anemone (Cerianthus membranaceus) is commonly found in all shaded areas of the reef as well as in caves and caverns. Sensitive to light and pressure, they are difficult to approach and nearly always retreat after a single photographic flash.

This is a gently sloping dive, often used for training purposes, with visibility improving the further you move out from the bay. The sandy seabed here is interspersed with large boulders and small beds of Posidonia. There are small shoals of two-banded bream (Diplodus vulgaris) and saddled bream (Oblada melanura) to be seen.

2 XWEJNI BAY

★★★

Location: To the northwest of Xwejni Bay.
Access: Directly off the beach and the small concrete platforms.
Conditions: This is a small, sheltered inlet and is always popular with locals and children, so expect it to be busy.
Average depth: 9m (30ft)
Maximum depth: 12m (40ft)
Average visibility: 15m (50ft)

There is a very shallow shore entry over small banks of Posidonia leading down to a series of rocky passageways. A mixture of algal 'fuzz' covers the rocky surfaces around here. A small ledge then drops down to a sandy bottom and hundreds of small fissures and cracks are home to moray eels (Muraena helena) as well as the common octopus (Octopus vulgaris). This site is mostly used as a beginner's dive but, for those who are fit, keen and adventurous, the dive for the Twin Arches (Site 3) can be started at this location.

3 TWIN ARCHES (MARSALFORN REEF)

★★★★★

Location: Directly out from the headland north of Xwieni Bay, about 200m (220yd) offshore.
Access: 80m (87yd) north of Xwieni Bay to the corner. Can be reached by a very long snorkel swim, but access is better by boat.
Conditions: Will be totally blown out during any NW/N/NE/Easterly winds, so best to dive when it is flat and calm.
Average depth: 30m (100ft)
Maximum depth: 45m (150ft)
Average visibility: 45m (150ft)
This extended rocky headland carved by two large archways has prolific fish life. Entry is over very shallow water, dotted with hundreds of sea urchins – passing over the large areas of sea grass, you can often see cuttlefish, octopuses and numerous wrasse. Once you reach the start of the wall at around 14m (45ft), keep to the right and follow it until you reach the twin arches. The first, smaller archway starts at 20m (66ft) and directly beneath it is the larger one, stretching to the seabed 45m (150ft) below. Time is limited because of the depth, so cut diagonally back to the shore or to the waiting dive boat. The outer reef has barracuda and grouper, with small blennies, nudibranchs and anemones common in the shallows; the undersides of the shaded arches are covered in small, colourful sponges and golden cup corals (*Astroides calycularis*). If you continue around the coast to your right you will come across a few large caves cut into the cliff.

GURNARDS [*BIES*]

Flying gurnards (*Dactylopterus volitans*) are found in fairly shallow water of under 10m (33ft). They live on muddy, sandy and rocky bottoms, and when threatened extend their large fan-like pectoral fins and 'fly' out of danger. They tend to be seen in their lifelong mating pairs skimming over the surface of the sandy seabed or 'walking' over the seabed with their modified ventral fins. Despite their name, flying gurnards do not fly through the air, as do true flying fish.

4 ANCHOR REEF (LANDSLIDE)

★★★★★★★

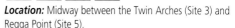

Location: Midway between the Twin Arches (Site 3) and Reqqa Point (Site 5).
Access: From the shore, left of a concrete fishing platform.
Conditions: Can be difficult if there is any surface surge. Entry is easy, but exit is trickier as you have to scramble up a steep rocky incline. Watch out for fishing lines.
Average depth: 12–30m (40–100ft)
Maximum depth: 45m (150ft)
Average visibility: 45m (150ft)
This is a very good snorkel dive along the edge of the shoreline, which affords some shelter. Thousands of small

Streaked Gurnard (Trigloporus lastoviza) can be found at Mgarr-ix-Xini (Site 24).

SHARKS [KELB IL-BAHAR]

Unlike in other areas of the world, sharks are very rarely seen in the Mediterranean. There are historical records of great white sharks (*Carcharodon carcharias*) [*Kelb il-bahar abjad*], and fishermen often catch thresher sharks (*Alopias vulpinus*) [*Pixxivolpi*], but the most commonly seen member of the shark family is the harmless lesser-spotted dogfish (*Scylliorhinus canicula*) [*Gattarell tat-titek*], often found near reef walls or amidst *Posidonia*. Dogfish lay their 'mermaid's purse' egg cases on *Posidonia* and offshore sea fans, to which they are attached by hardened sticky tendrils.

5 REQQA POINT

★★★★★★★★

Location: Most northerly point of Gozo, a small curved low spur which juts out into the sea.

Access: Along the rocky, bumpy coastal route next to the salt pans.

Conditions: Can be choppy, making entry and exit difficult. This site is also very popular with fishermen.

Average depth: 25m (80ft)

Maximum depth: Beyond 70m (230ft)

Average visibility: 45m (150ft)

Depending on the surge, access is either to the right or left of the headland, but the dive is conducted by swimming around the headland to the left, or west. This wall is near vertical in many places and cut by numerous fissures, caves and crevices. Snorkelling is popular along the wall because of the dramatic location and the numerous small fish. There are fishermen here so exercise caution.

sand smelt (*Antherina hespetus*) and damselfish (*Chromis chromis*) are to be seen. Grouper are common, as are various species of bream, and wrasse patrol the reef edge while small groups of parrotfish (*Sparisoma cretense*) nibble at the corals and hydroids. These fish are perhaps the most brightly coloured of all the fish found around the Maltese archipelago. The dive is down and along the steeply sloping wall to either the right or left, where you will find cardinalfish in every crevice (*Apogon imberbis*) and several species of scorpionfish nestling amongst the algae.

Divers fly along a wall with the aid of underwater scooters.

On the submarine section of the headland, two chimneys or holes drop down through the wall. To the right of the sheltered inlet there is a chimney that drops through the reef from 6m to 16m (20–52ft), while on the headland there is another much more serious chimney, to be dived only by very experienced divers. Diving this deep is not necessary, however, as there is so much marine life in the shallows, including Shrimps Cave, a shallow hollow in the cliff wall, filled with several species of shrimp.

6 BILLINGHURST CAVE
★★★★

Location: To the west of Reqqa Point and into the deeply indented corner of the shoreline, where you can see the entrance to the cave.
Access: Entry is possible by a 2m (6ft) jump and swim underwater to the cave; the exit is at Reqqa Point.
Conditions: There can be some serious surge in the cave and it should only be dived by experienced divers in flat, calm conditions.
Average depth: 20m (66ft)
Maximum depth: 35m (115ft)
Average visibility: 25m (80ft); torchlight needed
The cave has very little natural light and a dip in the middle further cuts off the daylight. The sides of the tunnel are pitted and eroded by the pounding sea and covered in a multitude of differently coloured sponges. There is less marine life than may be imagined, but after a 50m (55yd) swim you can surface inside the cave and cast your lights over the vaulted natural stone ceiling. The sight of blue open water with the sun shining through from the outer reef on the way out comes as something of a relief.

7 THE BLUE DOME (GHASRI VALLEY) (CATHEDRAL CAVE)
★★★★★★★★★

Location: Between Reqqa Point and Forna Point, a very distinctive deep winding cut in the headland.

SAND WRASSE [*TIRDA*]

Sand wrasse such as the rainbow wrasse (*Coris julis*) [*Gharusa*] and the ornate or Turkish wrasse (*Thalassoma pavo*) [*Lhudi*] live around rocks and algal beds and are easily spotted due to their bright colours and incessant curiosity, always accompanying divers wherever they go. These fish start life as females, but in a large group the biggest of the females undergoes a sex change, accompanied by a complete colour transformation, and gradually a 'supermale' emerges with a harem of females. When the male dies or is eaten the next largest female begins the process of gender change all over again.

HYDROIDS/JELLYFISH [*BRAMA*]

Jellyfish and hydroids are closely related to corals and anemones. The jellyfish is essentially a free-swimming form of the same type of creature as the hydroid, commonly called a medusa. The common or moon jellyfish (*Aurelia aurita*) is one of the few animals to be found in every ocean of the world, occurring in large aggregations during the spring and autumn plankton blooms. Cassiopeia (*Cotylorhiza tuberculata*) come into the islands in huge numbers during the summer months. Measuring over 30cm (12in) in circumference, they are covered in jewel-like warty tubercles and make excellent photographic subjects.

Access: Can be done from the shore, but requires an arduous climb (particularly after it has rained, when the valley silts up very quickly), over rock and down steps and then a long snorkel swim. Best done by dive boat.
Conditions: Sheltered inlet ideal for all levels of diver.
Average depth: 12m (in cave) to 30m (40–100ft)
Maximum depth: 30m (100ft)
Average visibility: 25m (80ft)
This dive is best started on the right-hand side of a steeply sloping wall, which drops down underwater to a huge cluster of large, rounded boulders covered in algae, sea urchins and brilliantly coloured starfish (*Ophidiaster ophidianus*). The shallows are also home to huge numbers of damselfish (*Chromis chromis*) and it was here that we spotted our first seahorse (*Hippocampus ramulosus*) in the Maltese islands, almost perfectly camouflaged among the spiky algae. The best part of this dive, however, is the cave itself. The entrance is only 5m (17ft) below the surface and leads you through to a huge domed vault, where you can surface and chat about your dive. As the dome extends above water level, there is no danger here of your exhalations disrupting marine species on the ceiling. Although there are few fish in the cave, the walls are covered in delicate corals, hydroids, sponges and golden zoanthids (*Parazoanthus axinellae*). The interior of the cave's seabed is covered in massive boulders and the view to the outside blue of the ocean is breathtaking, perfect for diver-silhouette photographs.

8 TA' CAMMA
★★★★★★★

Location: Around the corner running northeast from San Dimitri Point to a series of sheltered caves cut deep into the headland.
Access: By boat only.
Conditions: Facing north, this is an exposed site, so it can be choppy and is always in the shade due to the height of the cliffs.
Average depth: 25m (80ft)
Maximum depth: 40m (130ft)
Average visibility: 15m (50ft)

The most common of all the crustacean species to be found around the Maltese islands are hermit crabs, members of the family Paguridae and very similar to other decapods in this large family. Generally growing to a few centimetres in size, hermit crabs are armoured only on the outer half of their body, while the carapace or head is similar to many species of shrimp, albeit more heavily armoured and with more spiny protrusions. The inner half of the abdomen is long and soft, asymmetrical, unprotected and twisted to follow the coil of its shelly home. The hermit crab has a strong muscle, which it uses to retract the upper body parts into a discarded mollusc shell for protection.

MOBILE HOMES

These opportunistic small crustaceans are forever foraging on the seabed and rocky reefs, scavenging for any detritus or tasty morsel they can find. They carry their

Hermit crabs carry their mobile home with them to protect their soft inner parts.

mobile homes on their back and will rob other hermit crabs of their homes as they grow larger, often changing shells several times each day.

Of the seven species found in Maltese waters, one of the most common is the red reef hermit (*Dardanus arrosor*). It is wary of divers and retreats into its home whenever they get too close for comfort. A comparatively large hermit crab, it has warty tubercles on its claws and larger legs as well as delicate hair-like spines. It can be very aggressive towards neighbours and is constantly changing its shell.

The spider hermit crab (*Pagarus anachoretus*) is a smaller species, living in discarded cerith or whelk shells. Mostly reddish brown in colour, with lighter stripes on the smooth legs and claws, it is rather hairy in appearance, with strikingly green eyes.

The smallest species is the tubular hermit crab (*Carcinus tubularis*). With distinctive red spots on its white pointed claws and bluish tinged legs, this little creature is often found in cowrie shells and thin-lipped cone shells, for which its narrow body is best suited.

THE DECORATOR HERMIT

The largest of the hermit crabs is the giant hermit or decorator hermit (*Dardanus calidus*), which can grow up to 12cm (4½in). This crustacean requires a much larger and heavier shell for its home than the others, often using triton shells (*Charonia* spp.) or giant tun shells (*Tonna galea*). It also places a parasitic anemone called *Calliactis parasitica* on its shell, often two or three at a time, which it uses for additional protection. The crab and the anemone exist

The red reef hermit (Dardanus arrosor) never ceases searching for its next shell home.

in a truly symbiotic relationship, the former feeding small scraps of food to the anemone which, in return, provides a protective shroud against any potential predators such as small fish.

Hermit crabs perform a vital link in the marine ecosystem by scavenging decaying matter on the seabed. Moreover, they make excellent photographic subjects.

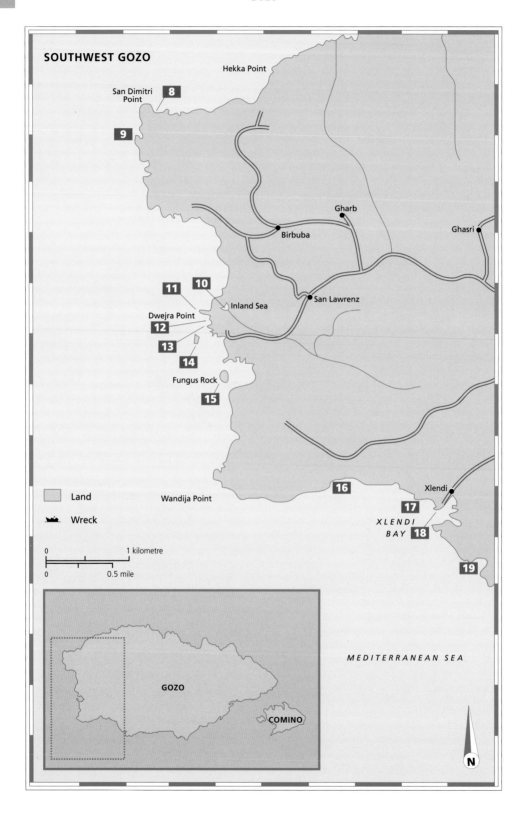

SOUTHWEST GOZO

Hekka Point

San Dimitri
Point   **8**

9

Gharb

Birbuba

Ghasri ●

11   **10**

Inland Sea   ● San Lawrenz

Dwejra Point
12

13

14

Fungus Rock

15

Land

Wandija Point

16   Xlendi ●

17

*XLENDI
BAY*   **18**

Wreck

19

0   1 kilometre

0   0.5 mile

MEDITERRANEAN SEA

GOZO

COMINO

N

Ta' Camma is a series of fives caverns cut deeply into the headland. Cavern One to the right has two entrances – one shallow at 9m (30ft), the other at 25m (80ft) – and two inner chambers, where shrimps and slipper lobsters can be found. Travelling left (east), the second chamber is very narrow and only accessible underwater; it is reminiscent of the Inland Sea (Site 10). The third chamber is large enough for a dive boat to travel in on the surface. The vertical sides drop over 30m (100ft) and are covered in small sponges, golden cup corals and spiral tubeworms. Caverns Four and Five are like the others, steep sided and covered in marine life. Perhaps the best aspect of all these caverns is the view of the beautiful blue coloured sea as you turn to exit each cavern. A superb dive site!

9 SAN DIMITRI POINT
★ ★ ★ ★ ★ ★ ★ ★

Location: Just south of San Dimitri Point, the most westerly point on Gozo.
Access: By boat only.
Conditions: Can be difficult with surface chop and current; only dive in flat calm waters and an easterly wind.
Average depth: 25m (80ft)
Maximum depth: Beyond 60m (200ft)
Average visibility: 50m (165ft)
A shallow reef juts out from a sheltered spike off the headland, where the dive boat is able to anchor in 6m (20ft). This reeftop is perfect for completing any timed safety stops at the end of your dive. The first part of the drop-off is quite gentle, after which you come to some house-sized boulders with vertical walls. Head out due west in open water – you will come across a couple of massive shoals of barracuda (*Sphyraena sphyraena*) – then turn back into the wall, which curves around to the south. Grouper are common, as are dentex, with thousands of damselfish and large shoals of saupe (*Sarpa salpa*), which feed on the algae-covered boulders. On the inside of the rocky ledge there is a very sheltered gully, filled with marine life, between the reef platform and the shore.

10 INLAND SEA
★ ★ ★ ★ ★ ★ ★

Location: At Dwejra Point head down to the right to the small enclosed bay in front of the fishing huts and small snack bar.
Access: From the shore, swim out on the surface then drop down immediately at the corner of the left-hand side to avoid the constant boat traffic carrying tourists through this dramatic headland.
Conditions: Must be done when the water is crystal clear,

as the inner bay silts up completely after heavy rain and this carries on through the water column to the other side of the headland, making diving conditions near impossible.
Average depth: 18m (60ft)
Maximum depth: 25–60m (80–200ft)
Average visibility: 30m (100ft); torch recommended
When conditions are perfect this is a fantastic dive along a narrow canyon that stretches 80m (260ft) through the headland to open water beyond. Boats whizz overhead, but the wall is so deep, vertical and underhanging for the most part that there is no danger of collision other than at the beginning of the dive and the end, assuming you exit in the same place. The view as you look out into the deep indigo blue of the open ocean is spectacular. Around the corner to both the right and left there are further vertical fissures in the cliff face which can be explored at all levels and are covered in marine life. These routes out to the left or right of the Inland Sea are not to be missed.

11 AZURE WINDOW (DWEJRA POINT)
★ ★ ★ ★ ★ ★ ★ ★

Location: Underneath the tip of Dwejra Point, a very obvious natural archway.
Access: Can be done by boat, but more popularly done by access through the Blue Hole (Site 12).
Conditions: Can have oceanic surge when weather is rough, but little current.
Average depth: 20–35m (66–115ft)
Maximum depth: Beyond 60m (200ft)
Average visibility: 45m (150ft)
The site gets its name from the underwater view as you look upwards to the natural arch above the surface, which reflects the azure blue as if you were looking through a massive window. Large boulders lie underneath the archway where they have fallen from above (which is somewhat disconcerting), but the marine life is prolific and the rocky surfaces are covered in spiny starfish (*Marthasterias glacialis*) and dotted everywhere with tiny

BARRACUDA [LIZZ]

Comparatively rare in most areas of the Mediterranean, one of the largest of the silvery predators around these islands is the great barracuda (*Sphyraena sphyraena*). This aggressive-looking fish swims in large shoals as a juvenile, then is often found near caverns and in smaller hunting packs as it gets older. Adult barracuda can grow up to 1.8m (6ft) and become solitary hunters, hiding underneath boats at anchor and preying on all species of fish – even their own kind. A large shoal of barracuda can always be encountered at San Dimitri Point off Gozo.

tube worms (*Bispira vulticornis*). Damselfish, wrasse, parrotfish and many different species of bream can be found along the walls, while deeper down amongst the large boulders on the seabed you can see the dusky grouper (*Epinephelus guaza*), recognizable by the yellow fringe on its dorsal fin. This is an incredibly scenic dive, as is the entire area, and divers tend to travel around the headland and back to the Blue Hole.

12 THE BLUE HOLE AND THE CHIMNEY
★★★★★★★★★

Location: Directly in front of the Azure Window (Site 11), at the bottom of Dwejra Point.
Access: Reached via a fairly difficult walk over ancient coralline limestone. The rough path leads you down to the shore, where a shallow-water shelf leads to the right where the Blue Hole is formed.

BASSLETS [*PIXXIROZA*]

The marine goldfish, sometimes known as the swallowtail seaperch (*Anthias anthias*), is a strikingly attractive fish that is very rare by Mediterranean standards. They are usually found in recesses and under shaded areas of the reef, seldom venturing further afield. Large numbers are located at the entrance to the Coral Cave and in the cave underneath the Blue Hole on Gozo, but they are scarce elsewhere.

False coral (Myriapora truncata) is delicate and can easily be dislodged by a misplaced fin.

Conditions: Sheltered at most times in the hole, as it is protected by a fringe of rock.
Average depth: 20m (66ft)
Maximum depth: 45m (150ft)
Average visibility: 45m (150ft)
The Blue Hole is a natural rock formation carved out over the centuries by wind and wave power. Offering a sheltered entry for a number of dives, this site includes a huge archway which starts at 8m (27ft) and has a flat top, almost square in shape, and covered in golden cup corals (*Parazoanthus axinellae*). A large cave also worth exploring can be found at the bottom of the hole. This dive then leads you round to the left (west), until you reach a fissure in the near-vertical wall. This opens up at around 6m (20ft); directly ahead of you is another, much smaller hole that is perfect for photography. Exit by retracing your route to the Blue Hole or the flat reef just to the left of the Blue Hole headland. This site is very popular late in the day, so get there early (before 09.30) to have the place to yourself.

13 CORAL CAVE
★★★★★

Location: To the left of the headland before you continue on the path down to the Blue Hole at Dwejra Point.
Access: From the shore, follow the fault line to the left

past the old sea-carved salt pans until you reach the water's edge. You must negotiate a 2m (6ft) jump into the water, but you are directly above the coral cave.

Conditions: Can be choppy on the surface.
Average depth: 25m (80ft)
Maximum depth: 30m (100ft)
Average visibility: 45m (150ft)

The entry may initially appear difficult, but is actually the best way to dive the site and allows for a maximum time in the cave. Its huge semi-circular opening has a sandy bottom inside and a tumble of boulders under the entrance. The silty sand slopes up to around 21m (70ft), where large burrowing anemones can be found (*Cerianthus membranaceus*). The entrance to the cavern also has large numbers of quite rare marine goldfish (*Anthias anthias*). Turning right, or north, you come to a vertical wall which drops to 30m (100ft); this is home to hermit crabs, starfish, tube worms and small, colourful scorpionfish (*Scorpaena notata*). Painted comber (*Serranus scriba*) are everywhere, as are parrotfish, amberjacks, wrasse and damselfish. Bristle or fireworms (*Hermodice carunculata*) are also prevalent, and you should take care to avoid contact with them. The exit is via the Blue Hole.

14 CROCODILE ROCK
★★★★★★

Location: The crocodile-shaped, low-lying rock just offshore between Dwejra Point and Fungus Rock.

RAYS [*HAMIEMA*]

The eagle ray (*Myliobatis aquila*) [*Hamiema komuni*] can be found in deep water along the edges of walls, particularly off Crocodile Rock and Fungus Rock in Gozo. This large ray has a snout somewhat like that of a pig, which it uses to dig and forage beneath the sand for crustaceans and molluscs. The electric or torpedo ray (*Torpedo marmorata*) [*Haddiela komuni*] is much smaller in size, growing to a length of around 1m (3ft). The rounded body has two electrical organs with which it stuns its prey. Thornback rays (*Raja clavata*) [*Raja tal-fosos*] are more common and can be found in shallow water all round the coastline, growing to a maximum of 1m (3ft). They are roughly diamond in shape, with spiny protuberances along the backbone and tail.

Access: By boat and from the rocky shore.
Conditions: Can be choppy on the surface, with surge and slight current along the outer wall.
Average depth: 35m (115ft)
Maximum depth: 45m (150ft)
Average visibility: 45m (150ft)

The dive boat anchors on the top of the rocky reef between Crocodile Rock and the shore, where the depth is around 7m (24ft). The rock platform here is deeply grooved and covered in several species of marine algae, including *Padina povonia* and *Udotea petiolata*. Following the reef to the southern edge of the rock,

---

Cuttlefish such as this Sepia officinalis are regularly seen near algal beds.

there is a natural amphitheatre with near-vertical sides. Continuing around to the right, there are a number of deeply incised fissures; the bottom of the wall gives way to a steeply sloping seabed of huge algae-covered boulders. Grouper are common in this area, as are large shoals of salema (*Sarpa salpa*). The exit is by retracing your route, but in much shallower water, all the way around the rock, or by following the largest fissure up to the shallow reef platform, where the dive boat can be located.

15 FUNGUS ROCK
★★★★★

Location: The huge rock offshore at the entrance to Dwejra Bay.
Access: By boat.
Conditions: Sheltered on the inside, but can be choppy with surge and a slight current on the outer wall.
Average depth: 30m (100ft)
Maximum depth: Beyond 60m (200ft)
Average visibility: 45m (150ft)

This massive lump of limestone has a hole running through its northern part. Underwater, the scenery is as dramatic as above, with vertical walls, fissures, gulleys and caverns created by boulders lying against one another. The walls are covered in algae, sea urchins, tube worms, starfish, bristle worms and sea potatoes (*Halocinthya papillosa*), their brilliant red colour always catching the eye. This area is fished actively, so there are few fish other than damselfish, but further out in deeper water eagle rays and large jacks are seen regularly.

16 ZURZIEP REEF
★★★★★★

Location: Midway between Wardija Point and Xlendi Bay.
Access: By boat only.
Conditions: Can be choppy on the surface, with only slight current.

SNAILS [*BEBBUX TAL-BAHAR*]

The mollusc family is well represented in the Maltese islands, with a wide diversity of members, including octopus, squid, cuttlefish and nudibranchs. The file clam (*Lima lima*) hides in crevices in the cliff walls and can be noticed by its long tentacles, which are used to ward off predators. Cowries are rare (*Cypraea spurca* and *Cypraea lurida*). Their protective body parts or mantle fold up around the body of the shell, giving it a wonderful sheen. Common whelks (*Buccinum corneum*) and common cerith (*Cerithium vulgatum*) are found everywhere and in all habitats.

Average depth: 21m (70ft)
Maximum depth: Beyond 30m (100ft)
Average visibility: 50m (165ft)

This dive is best done in the afternoon, when the sun swings over to the west. The dive boat anchors in 6m (20ft). There is a platform of rock at the base of the cliff, only 5m (17ft) underwater, where the St Andrew's Divers Cove mooring buoy is located. When conditions are right, there is the opportunity for an interesting snorkel along the edge of the platform and the vertical wall. This area is rarely fished and shoals of bream are found here as well as large numbers of amberjacks, parrotfish, wrasse, damselfish and sand smelt. There are plenty of shallow caves which host cardinalfish and various species of anemone.

17 ULYSSES CAVE
★★★★

   ☑

Location: West of Xlendi Bay, outside the bay and around to the first huge cavern carved out of the vertical cliffs.
Access: By boat only.
Conditions: Can have surge in the cave, so best done when the sea is calm.
Average depth: 25m (80ft)
Maximum depth: 45m (150ft)
Average visibility: 25m (80ft)

The area is popular with fishermen, so there are no large schools of fish here, but this site makes an excellent night dive as there is a whole host of colourful marine life to be discovered in the light of your torch beam. The rocky platform to the left of the cave makes an ideal landing place while you gather your equipment together. The shallow wall is covered in brilliant green algae interspersed with purple crustose algae (*Pseudolithophyllum expansum*) and false coral (*Myriapora truncata*). Brilliant red scorpionfish are easily picked out, as are the bright yellow dots of the golden zoanthids. A small cave to the right of the larger opening leads to an area where natural fresh water mixes with sea water, creating a misty blue halocline. Some quite beautiful rock formations are to be found here.

LOBSTERS [*AWWISTA*]

Slipper lobsters (*Scyllarides latus*) and spiny lobsters (*Palinurus elephas*) are very rare. They inhabit the rocky reef ledges and always hide from direct sunlight, actively foraging at night and retreating rapidly by fast movements of the tail, which propel them backwards. The common lobster (associated more with the North Sea) is also rare, having been fished commercially for many years. They can still be found in the winter months when the water temperature cools down and they come up out of the deep water.

Above: *Preferring deeper caves and rocky reefs, the pen shell is becoming rare in Maltese waters.*
Below: *Gobies like this Gobius cruenatus are difficult to photograph and require great patience.*

18 XLENDI CAVE AND REEF
★★★★

Location: To the northern corner of Xlendi Bay, through the headland and onto the outer reef.
Access: The preferred entry for this shore dive is to jump in from a raised platform past the St Andrew's Divers Cove shop. From here, swim across the bay on the surface until you find the entrance to the cave – just below where the bright green plants can be found on the otherwise bare limestone wall.
Conditions: Sheltered, but very busy with boat traffic and swimmers.
Average depth: 6m (20ft)
Maximum depth: 25m (80ft)
Average visibility: Very variable in the cave from 6 to 30m (20–100ft)
The tunnel through the headland is only 2m (6ft) deep in Xlendi Bay and 6m (20ft) on the other side, so it is possible to snorkel through. From here dive to the left to the gentle outer drop-off and around the reef, which extends underwater from the headland. Part of this forms a pinnacle, now marked by a navigation Cardinal Point. The cave is more popular at night as it is a nice easy dive in shallow water – it is also popular with less experienced divers, and is many's first cave adventure. The cave walls are brilliantly coloured with golden zoanthids, red starfish and sponges, green and purple algae, and there are bristle worms everywhere. During the winter months a small school of juvenile barracuda seeks shelter at the entrance.

19 DAWRA TAS-SANAP
★★★★★

Location: The first large sheltered inlet to the southeast of Xlendi Bay.
Access: By boat only.
Conditions: Sheltered, but there can be surge against the cliff face and cave.
Average depth: 20m (66ft)
Maximum depth: 45m (150ft)
Average visibility: 50m (165ft)
This is a deep cave and natural arch eroded from the surrounding cliffs, with a massive semi-circular cavern at the base of the archway as you travel south in around 20m (66ft). The wall drops off very steeply and there are large schools of saddled bream (*Oblada melanura*) and salema (*Sarpa salpa*). The bottom of the arch has some massive boulders covered in colourful sponges, with ornate wrasse (*Thalassoma pavo*) forming small hunting groups and the juveniles 'cleaning up' after other fish species. The wall again becomes vertical as you swim around to the bay on your left (with the usual sightings of dentex and grouper).

It becomes much shallower here and you can regularly find spiny lobsters (*Palinurus elephas*). The entrance of the cave next to the cliff face is absolutely covered in marine life.

20 TA' CENC CLIFFS
★★

Location: Underneath the vertical cliffs which face due west, to the west of Newwiela Point.
Access: By boat only.
Conditions: Exposed to southwesterly swells and can be done only when the sea is flat calm.
Average depth: 20m (66ft)
Maximum depth: 35m (115ft)
Average visibility: 45m (150ft)
Beneath the vertical cliff, a small submarine platform juts out from the headland at 8m (27ft) deep. It allows for safe boat anchorage and is a perfect location to do a safety decompression stop, since this is a deep dive around the wall of the reef platform. The area is overfished, so only shoals of damselfish and small groups of bream, a few grouper, lobster and parrotfish are to be found. The walls are covered in algae, with bristle worms, sea urchins and lots of starfish.

21 NEWWIELA POINT
★★★★

Location: On the eastern side of Newwiela Point.
Access: By boat only.
Conditions: Generally sheltered, but there can be surge from the southeast.
Average depth: 25m (80ft)
Maximum depth: Beyond 35m (117ft)
Average visibility: 45m (150ft)

THE MALTESE SHARKS

Actually the British Sub Aqua Club's Branch No. 1818, the Sharks were formed in 1984 by a group of very experienced expatriate divers who were living and working in the Maltese islands.

The main aim of the Sharks is to dive at different and new locations throughout the year, and they have been responsible for establishing numerous less accessible dive sites around the islands. They are also happy to train new members and visitors. The Sharks have a large and eventful social calendar, and visiting divers are warmly invited to join them for a dive.

In addition an active marine conservation group has now been formed to liaise with the Department of Tourism and assist in the development of marine reserves around the islands. For more information contact: Dave Foote, tel (356) 21666837; Julian Christians, tel (356) 21214055, e-mail jules@melita.net. www.xdive.co.uk/sharks.

Several of the most popular dive sites in the Maltese islands are concentrated around Dwejra Point at the western end of Gozo. This fascinating area is notable not only for its underwater features. In the 17th century, one of a series of fortified towers on Gozo was built at Dwejra Point, partly to add to the line of coastal defence and also to guard Fungus Rock.

FUNGUS ROCK
Originally named 'Il-Gebla Tal-General' (The General's Rock), this huge mass of limestone got its more common name from a small, rare shrub-like fungus that was discovered here by the Knights of St John. The Maltese Fungus (*Cynomorium coccineum*) – which grows up to 18cm (7in) – was used as a remedy against haemorrhages, dysentery and ulcers as well as staunching blood flow and guarding against infection. Known by the Arabs as the 'treasure of drugs', Fungus Rock was guarded closely by the Knights, who built an early form of cable car to the mainland (divers can still see the hole through which the cable ran).

The shallow lagoon behind Fungus Rock (Qala Dwejra) is today favoured by snorkellers and small pleasure craft, which camp out in the bay. North of Fungus Rock is Crocodile Rock, named for its crocodile-shaped 'snout' when seen from the shore. Further north again,

Dwejra Point is dominated by the Azure Window, a massive natural arch which stretches underwater and which is a popular dive site (Site 11). In front of the arch, another natural formation in the ironstone shore is the Blue Hole (Site 12).

The Blue Hole offers safe entry for divers on this exposed headland and is the entry and exit point for three different dives. The hole has been eroded by weather, tide and freshwater run-off, and is connected to the open sea by a spectacular underwater arch. The entry over the sharp rocks and ancient salt pans is studded with fossils.

INLAND SEA
In fact, this entire headland is a mass of ancient fossils and is dissected by huge vertical fault lines, which have been eroded into canyons and caverns. The largest of these connects into the Inland Sea, where there are some fishermen's huts. Above the village is a chapel dedicated to St Anne, constructed in 1963 on the site of three earlier chapels, now demolished. A nearby cave discovered in 1729 once held a statue of a golden calf mounted on a solid gold pedestal, and led to a popular belief that Gozo was a sacred island.

Dwejra Point is a superb historical site as well as one of the best diving locations in the islands.

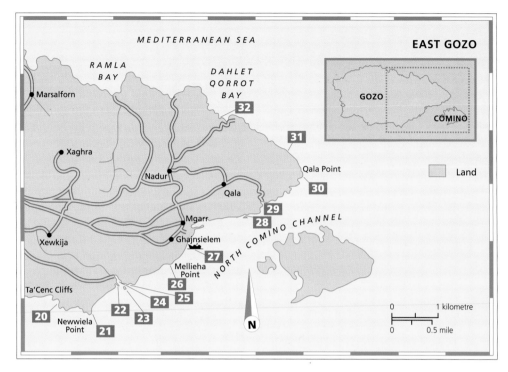

This is a steep drop-off and wall with some areas covered in huge boulders, offering interesting places to spot grouper. There are small caverns all over the site with two separate underwater archways, one negotiable by divers, the other too small, though it makes for interesting photographs. Huge numbers of damselfish are found here, mostly juveniles, which are royal blue. Octopus and moray eels are quite common and their lairs can be spotted fairly easily by the shell and crab debris littering the foreground.

22 TA' CENC 21/03/08
★★★★

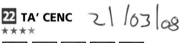

Location: From the private rock platform near Mgarr ix-Xini belonging to the Ta' Cenc Hotel.
Access: At the bottom of 103 steps from the car park to the water's edge. Permission should be sought from the hotel management.
Conditions: Sheltered bay, can silt up after heavy rain.
Average depth: 25m (80ft)
Maximum depth: 35m (115ft)
Average visibility: 30m (100ft)
Swim across the entrance of the small bay and dive on the wall, turning around to your right (northwest). The canyon on the way out is littered with huge boulders, gradually giving way to a steeply sloping wall covered in algae and all the associated marine inhabitants, such as rainbow wrasse (*Coris julis*), longsnout wrasse (*Symphodus*

doderleini) and Bucchichi's goby (*Gobius bucchichii*). To the left of the entry point there is also an attractive cave. This site is best visited on a night dive, when a wider and more colourful variety of marine life becomes visible.

23 FESSEJ ROCK (BLACK ROCK)
★★★★★

Location: Offshore from the Mgarr ix-Xini inlet along the south shore near Mgarr harbour.
Access: By boat only.
Conditions: An exposed location which can be choppy, with surge and current.
Average depth: 30m (100ft)
Maximum depth: 50m (165ft)
Average visibility: 30m (100ft)
Rising about 15m (50ft) above the water, Fessej Rock plunges vertically to the seabed 50m (165ft) below, amidst a tumble of huge boulders. Anchorage is by placing a chain around a small rocky outcrop close to the water's edge. Although this is always undertaken as a deep dive, because of the vertical formation of the rock, divers of all levels and even snorkellers are able to enjoy the delights of a vertical wall dive amidst large schools of fish. Essentially the dive is around the rock, descending and ascending in a spiral to bring you back to the boat's mooring. There are large tube worms (*Sabella spallanzani*) and squat lobsters (*Munida rugosa*), and divers are followed by groups of

dentex (*Dentex dentex*) and amberjacks (*Seriola dumerili*). Barracuda, tuna and grouper as well as octopus and other lobster can also be found on this dive.

24 MGARR IX-XINI 20/03/08
★★★★★

Location: At the Mgarr ix-Xini inlet, around towards the private beach for the Ta' Cenc Hotel.
Access: From the beach at the end of the inlet.
Conditions: Sheltered and easy dive with little boat traffic, but popular with swimmers.
Average depth: 6m (20ft)
Maximum depth: 14m (47ft)
Average visibility: 15m (50ft)
This dive is very popular with photographers due to the huge variety of fish species – flying gurnard (*Dactylopterus volitans*), stargazers (*Uranoscopus scaber*), picarel (*Spicara flexuosa*) and even seahorses (*Hippocampus ramulosus*). There is an interesting cave about 100m (330ft) along the right-hand wall in 14m (45ft), which extends quite far in and has a sharp narrow twist to the left at the end. This entrance has lots of tiny holes and crevices with delicate lacy bryozoans (*Reteporella septentrionalis*) and lightbulb tunicates (*Clavelina lepadiformis*). You can surface inside the cave. The sheltered valley and shallow depths make the site very popular for night dives, and you will always find octopuses, burrowing starfish (*Astropecten aranciacus*) and razorfish (*Xyrichthys novacula*), which hide under the sand when you approach them.

25 RAS IL-_OBZ (THE FINGER) (MIDDLE FINGER)
★★★★★

Location: East of Fessej Rock to small headland and two sheltered bays that jut out from the shore.
Access: By boat, but it can be reached by car down a rough farm track.
Conditions: Liable to surge from the south, with current expected off the pinnacle.
Average depth: 30m (100ft)
Maximum depth: 48m (160ft)
Average visibility: 25m (80ft)
This site was once the former location of the sewerage outfall (which has now been moved elsewhere) and is therefore now open to divers. Ras il-_obz is a single pinnacle which rises vertically out of the seabed just 12m (40ft) off the headland. As it nears its summit at 11m (36ft) the rock splits into two and you can usually find lobsters, slipper lobsters and octopus in the fissure. The rock is covered in algae growth dotted with spiral tubeworms (*Spirographis spallanzani*). Schools of chromis, bogue and

smelt are found all around the rock, preyed upon by painted comber (*Serranus scriba*). At the end of the dive, it is a short, easy swim in towards the shallow bays on either side of the headland, where you can enjoy the usual blennies, gobies and nudibranchs found in these depths.

26 XATT L-AHMAR
★★★★

Location: Southwest of Mgarr in the bay, sheltered by the curving headland of Mellieha Point.
Access: Can be done by boat, but more generally from the shore over farming land and an easy walk down, with numerous entry and exit points.
Conditions: Generally sheltered with little current.
Average depth: 9m (30ft)
Maximum depth: 30m (100ft)
Average visibility: 30m (100ft)
The dive is around to the right of the rocky ledge which extends underwater and drops down from 9m (30ft) to 21m (70ft), where jumbles of boulders create small swimthroughs and shaded areas, with thriving golden zoanthids and false corals. As always, the rocky surfaces are covered in a dense mat of algae, where green wrasse (*Labrus viridus*), sharpsnout bream (*Diplodus puntazzo*) and bearded scorpionfish (*Scorpaena scrofa*) can be found. There is a proposal to sink a ship here as an artificial reef.

27 WRECK XLENDI
★★★

Location: South of Ghajnsielem, west of Mgarr Harbour.
Access: By boat, but it can be reached by car down a rough farm track. A new car park has also been created for divers' use, close to the water's edge, with a set of ladders to aid exit.
Conditions: Some surges from the south, but little current.
Average depth: 36m (120ft)
Maximum depth: 48m (160ft)
Average visibility: 25m (80ft)
The MV *Xlendi* was a roll-on, roll-off ferry, built in 1955 in

DEEP DIVING

Many sites around the Maltese islands count as deep dives, and the following precautions are sensible:
• Attend a deep diving course.
• Dive only with experienced deep divers.
• Increase depth slowly.
• Plan your dive and dive your plan.
• Do not put yourself or others at risk.
• If symptoms appear, ascend immediately until symptoms are relieved.

OCTOPUS AND SQUID [QARNITA U SICCA]

Of all invertebrate animals, octopus and squid have the most highly developed nervous systems and are often found prowling the reefs at night. Squid in particular appear fascinated by divers' lights and the obvious food attracted by them. Their bodies are covered in chromatophores, which enable them to change colour and blend completely into their surroundings. Octopuses are highly mobile and can squeeze through an aperture many times smaller than their own body size. The common octopus (*Octopus vulgaris*) and the white-spotted octopus (*Octopus macropus*) are seen on most night dives. Cuttlefish (*Sepia officinalis*) are found regularly amongst *Posidonia* beds. Although they share the octopus's ability to change colour and shape, they have an inflexible inner shell (a remnant of their mollusc heritage), which gives them less versatility.

Denmark and weighing 1,123 tons. She is 80m (262ft) long, 23m (75ft) high and 12m (39ft) wide. The *Xlendi* was acquired by Gozo Channel Company in 1970 and worked between Cirkewwa, Valletta and Mgarr Harbour, before finally being retired in 1997 during a cost-cutting exercise by the ferry company. The ship languished in Valletta harbour in Malta while negotiations took place as to her fate and finally, on 12 November 1999, the *Xlendi* slipped beneath the waves to become the latest in diver attractions. As a ferry, with both stern and bows identical, each with a propeller and rudder, it is difficult to say if she

is on her port or starboard side, but she is now lying at 45 degrees, parallel to the shoreline, her decks facing open water. Now partly supported by her funnel and collapsed masts, with a maximum depth of 41m (135ft), the cargo bay of the ship is open, but collapsing slowly; qualified divers only may be able to swim all the way through. This is a deep dive, but well worth the effort.

28 IL-GEBLA TAL-_ALFA (MGARR ROCK)
★★★★

Location: Inside the large sloping rock east of Mgarr harbour.
Access: By boat.
Conditions: Generally sheltered; used as a beginners' site.
Average depth: 8m (27ft)
Maximum depth: 18m (60ft)
Average visibility: 15m (50ft)
This large rock has often been likened to a wedge of Swiss cheese because of the huge number of caves, tunnels and holes that run through it. Most are in quite shallow water of around 8m (27ft). Large *Posidonia* beds can be found further out, but the main interest is around

The MV Xlendi is the latest addition to the popular shipwrecks of Malta, Comino and Gozo.

the caves, where schools of damselfish, sand smelt and bream vie for space. The caves contain large red starfish (*Ophidiaster ophidians*) and even featherstarfish or crinoids (*Antedon mediterranea*). Octopuses are common and moray eels (*Muraena helena*) are generally found.

29 HONDOQ BAY
★★★

Location: Hondoq Bay.
Access: Park by the water for easy access off the shore.
Conditions: Sheltered – used for beginners' dives only.
Average depth: 6m (20ft)
Maximum depth: 10m (33ft)
Average visibility: 7m (23ft)
This sandy-bottomed bay has lots of *Posidonia* and small fish. It is classed as a 'rummage dive' and you can find interesting hermit crabs, gobies and even cuttlefish. The bay (from where the water pipeline runs to Comino from Gozo) is not exactly awe-inspiring, but is loved by trainees, who often get their first feel for Mediterranean diving here. It is popular as a night dive and is one of the only sheltered sites when the wind blows from the northwest.

30 QALA
★★★

Location: Inside the sheltered inlet at Qala Point.
Access: By boat.
Conditions: Sheltered from the northeast winds.
Average depth: 12m (40ft)
Maximum depth: 15m (50ft)
Average visibility: 30m (100ft)
The seabed is of rough sand and so is not prone to silting, making the visibility better than in many surrounding areas. *Posidonia* banks are dotted all over and little boulders form micro-habitats for small, algae-covered spider crabs. Hermit crabs are common and there are large numbers of wrasse and bream. Cuttlefish are often found amidst the sea grasses or hidden in the sand. Sand divers (*Synodus saurus*) have been found as well as red mullet (*Mullus surmuletus*).

31 THE QUARRY (QALA)
★★★★

Location: North of the east point of Gozo.
Access: By boat only (road access through the quarry is no longer possible).
Conditions: Dependent on the northwest *Majjistral* wind.
Average depth: 15m (50ft)
Maximum depth: 30m (100ft)
Average visibility: 15m (50ft)

A shy coral shrimp (Stenopus spinosus) comes out to forage at night.

This sunken reef is generally used for training. Starting at around 6m (20ft), it gradually slopes down to around 30m (100ft), over algal growths of several seaweeds, hydroids, sea grasses, small fan worms and fireworms (*Hermodice carunculata*). These are dotted with small wrasse, blennies, sea urchins and damselfish. There are also three or four huge anchors amidst the jumble of boulders.

32 DAHLET QORROT
★★★

Location: To the west of Dahlet Qorrot Bay.
Access: From the shore.
Conditions: Generally sheltered except in the worst circumstances, with wind from the northeast. On the whole, this is an easy site suitable for beginners.
Average depth: 6m (20ft)
Maximum depth: 12m (40ft)
Average visibility: 10m (33ft)
This dive is mostly carried out as an introduction to diving. The site features large beds of neptune grass (*Posidonia oceanica*) amongst small sand patches, which are usually filled with grass detritus. The scenery is not exactly inspiring, but there are nearly always schools of green wrasse (*Labrus viridus*) and damselfish (*Chromis chromis*).

HOW TO GET THERE

By helicopter: There is an Air Malta helicopter link with the international airport on Malta. Arrangements can be made in advance through most of the better hotels or dive shops on the island as well as through your local travel agent at your point of booking.

By ferry: This is the most popular route, with trips daily every 45min from around 06:00 to after midnight. The service is run by the **Gozo Channel Company** and operates round the clock from June to September. Ferries depart from Cirkewwa on the northwesterly tip of Malta to Mgarr harbour on Gozo. Payment is made on the return trip from Gozo to Malta; a return ticket costs Lm 6.5 per car and driver, plus Lm 2 for each passenger. Advance booking is not necessary, but bear in mind that early morning ferries (before 09:00) are frequently full, as are those on Friday evenings, when crossings are often subject to delays.

GETTING AROUND

Most visitors **hire a car** on Malta and take it over to Gozo on the ferry. Finding your way around is relatively easy, as all main roads radiate out of the capital, Victoria.

GOZO LACE

The Maltese islands are renowned for their lace-making, much of the lace being produced in Gozo. When buying lace, be sure to check whether it is genuinely hand-made. Labels that say 'made by hand' may simply mean that the machine was hand-operated.

Each hand-made piece varies in style and tension, depending on the lace-maker's skill, and usually follows a stencilled pattern pinned to a lace-maker's pillow by means of bobbins. On traditionally hand-made lace, patterns usually include the Maltese Cross – a popular motif – as well as the sun, moon and the tree of life, designs that reflect the cosmopolitan composition of the original Knights of the Order of St John of Jerusalem. Black lace, favoured by Queen Victoria, is rarely worked now because black thread strains the eyes.

Remember that even the smallest piece of finished work represents hours of labour – a large tablecloth can take anything from a year to eighteen months to complete – so resist the temptation to haggle when buying.

Note that the one-way road system can be confusing in the city centre. Local car hire is available from **Victor J. Borg Enterprises**, tel (356) 21552908.

Local **buses** are rather haphazard, except for service No. 25, which connects Mgarr harbour at the ferry terminal with Victoria centre. **Taxis** are also available, though quite expensive.

WHERE TO STAY

The standard of hotels on Gozo is high and most have good restaurants. For those who prefer to self-cater there are converted farmhouses, which can sleep up to eight people; many have their own swimming pool as well. This type of accommodation is very popular and must be booked in advance, either through the local dive centres or from **Gozo Holidays**, Dunny Lane, Chipperfield, Hertfordshire WD4 9DQ, UK; tel (01923) 260919/fax (01923) 263482 e-mail: gozo.holidays@dial.pipex.com.

Calypso Hotel, Marsalforn, XRA 105 tel (356) 21562000/fax (356) 21562012 Plain in appearance, but good-sized rooms. Four restaurants including one Chinese. Situated on the waterfront with Calypso Divers. Parking can be a problem on the seafront.

Cornucopia Hotel, 10 Gnien Imrik St, Xaghra tel (356) 21552633/fax (356) 21552910 Farmhouse-style conversion with natural stone walls, fine wood furniture and lots of antiques. Attractive restaurant, two swimming pools.

St Patrick's Hotel, 12 Xlendi Seafront, Xlendi Bay tel (356) 21562951/fax (356) 21556598 Popular new hotel directly on the waterfront and next to St Andrew's Divers Cove dive centre. International restaurant and open-air café on the seafront.

Ta' Cenc Hotel, Sannat tel (356) 21556819/21556830/fax (356) 21558199 Outstanding 5-star hotel with a good reputation for food. Bungalow-style accommodation in extensive grounds near Sannat, two swimming pools. Private 'beach' (actually a rocky foreshore) with excellent diving.

WHERE TO EAT

Most visitors tend to eat in their hotel, where the food is generally very good, particularly the Friday night barbecue at Cornucopia, the pasta and lunches at St Patrick's, and the buffet nights at Ta' Cenc. However, for those who are self-catering or

who want to eat out, the following list offers a selection.

Auberge Chez Amand, Gharb Rd, Victoria tel (356) 21551197 Belgian cuisine in a rustic Gozitan setting.

Bonitos, Triq il-Madonna, Xlendi, Gozo tel (356) 21559 315/fax (356) 21566 364; e-mail info@herbeesbonitos.com. Friendly and relaxed with superb local seafood in an Italian style.

Jeffreys, Gharb Rd, Gharb tel (356) 21561006 Good value in a delightful rural setting; menu changes daily.

Mgarr ix-Xini Grill Bar, Mgarr ix-Xini, Gozo Contact Sandra & Noel tel (356) 21550208; mobile (356) 79854007 The best fresh, grilled seafood around.

Oleander Bar and Restaurant, 10 Victory Square, Xaghra tel (356) 21557230 Excellent local specialities, fresh fish, pasta, Maltese wines (try the *Frizzante*).

Ta' Frenc, Marsalforn Rd, Gozo tel (356) 21553888/fax (356) 21564271 Farmhouse-style conversion in lovely surroundings, reasonably priced with good food.

DIVE FACILITIES

There are ten registered diving operations on Gozo. For a full list, contact branches of the Maltese Tourist Office overseas (see page 16), or the Federation of Underwater Activities in Malta (FUAM), PO Box 29, Gzira, Malta.

Atlantis Diving School, Triq il-Qolla, Marsalforn, Gozo, VCT116; tel (356) 21554685/fax (356) 21555661; e-mail atlantis@digigate.net. **Blue Waters Dive Cove**, Triq il-Kuncizzjoni, Qala, Gozo, GSM103; tel/fax (356) 21565626; www.divebluewaters.com. **Calypso Diving Centre**, Marsalforn Bay Seafront, Marsalforn, Gozo VCT116; tel (356) 21561757/fax (356) 21562020; e-mail info@calypsodivers.com. **Frankie's Gozo Diving Centre**, Triq il-Imgarr, Xewkja, Gozo, VCT111; tel (356) 21551315/fax (356) 21560356; e-mail frankie@digigate.net. **Gozo Aquasports Dive Centre**, Triq il-Rabat, Marsalforn, Gozo, VCT116; tel (356) 21563037/fax (356) 21559938; www.gozoaquasports.com. **Moby Dives Training Facilities**, Tradewinds Building, Triq il-Gostra, Xlendi, Gozo VCT115; tel/fax (356) 21564429; e-mail moby@digigate.net. **Nautic Team Diving Centre**, Triq il-Vulkan, Marsalforn, Gozo,

XRA105; tel/fax (356) 21558507; www.nauticteam.com. **Scubatech Gozo Diving Centre**, 46A, Triq Marina, Marsalforn, Gozo, XRA105; tel/fax (356) 21561221; e-mail dive@scubatech.info. **St. Andrew's Divers Cove**, St. Simon Street, Xlendi, Gozo, VCT115; tel (356) 21551301/fax (356) 21561548; e-mail standrew@gozodive.com; www.gozodive.com. **Utina Diving College**, Triq ir-Rabat, Xlendi, Gozo, VCT115; tel (356) 21550514; e-mail utina@gozomail.com; www.utina.dk.

DIVERS' TREATMENTS

Higgi Cox is an experienced health practitioner, offering a range of treatments from Shiatsu to Acupuncture She has treated many diver related injuries. Contact Higgi on tel (356) 21566315/99216816; www.doinghealing.com.

FILM PROCESSING

Film is invariably sent the short distance to Malta for processing in the labs there.

EMERGENCIES

In an emergency, there is a heliport pad operated by Air Malta with direct links to the police, the nearest hospital and hyperbaric chamber on Malta. All decompression

accidents are ferried this way.

Emergency	tel 112
Hyperbaric Unit	tel (356) 21234766
Gozo General Hospital	tel (356) 21561600, (356) 21556851
St Luke's Hospital, Malta	tel (356) 21241251, (356) 21247860

LOCAL HIGHLIGHTS

In **Victoria** a visit to the Citadel, built AD870–1200 during Arab occupation, is a must. This fortified area, resembling a medieval castle, was built as a defence against frequent attacks by corsairs from the Barbary Coast. Today the Citadel is practically uninhabited and few of the original houses remain. Visitors are able to walk the ramparts (from where there are spectacular views) and wander through the ancient narrow streets, visiting souvenir shops where hand-made lace can be purchased. St Mary's Cathedral and several museums lie within the walls.

Ggantija ('the place of the giants') is possibly the most impressive and well preserved ancient temple site on the Maltese islands. Dating back to 3600–3200BC, the two temples are said to be among the oldest free-standing monuments in the world. Situated on the edge of a plateau, they are constructed from honey-coloured stone. The outer walls are made from coralline limestone, while the more workable, softer

globigerina limestone was used for the inner walls, built in alternating flat and projecting blocks for stability. Access is from Victoria Bus Terminus, Xaghra (buses 64 and 65).

You can visit the Gozo glass factory to watch local artisans blowing glass with skill and artistry. Morning visits are available; contact **Gozo Glass**, Crafts Village, San Lawrenz, Gozo; tel (356) 21561974/fax (356) 21560354. Another popular stop is Gozo Heritage on the outskirts of Mgarr, which has an exhibition of artefacts revealing the island's rich cultural history. Contact: **Gozo Heritage**, Victoria; tel (356) 21551475.

The *Gozo Princess* offers daily and sunset cruises from Xlendi Bay and Marsalforn to Fungus Rock and the Azure Window. Contact: **Xlendi Pleasure Cruises**, 'Casa Tartonio', Anici St, Victoria VCT 106; tel (356) 21559967/fax (356) 21555667. Boat trips through the **Inland Sea** are also popular, particularly appreciated if you have already swum underneath it.

TOURIST INFORMATION

Gozo Tourist Office, 1 Palm St, Victoria; tel (356) 21557047.

Xlendi Bay is a popular area with local Gozitans and has great shore diving (sites 17-19).

The Maltese islands offer some of the most scenic underwater caves and caverns in the Mediterranean. Although cave and cavern diving are similar in nature, there are important differences. A cave dive is generally into an area away from natural sunlight, using specialist equipment, and would include the penetration of some wrecks. Cavern diving is what the average visiting sports diver will experience when on the Maltese islands. Here divers explore the outer reaches of caves and do not venture away from the sunlight, always keeping the safe exit close at hand in case of emergency.

MALTESE CAVES AND CAVERNS

Many of the popular sites are on Comino and Gozo. Areas such as Marsalforn, Xlendi Bay and Dwejra Point on Gozo and the Comino caves are high on many visiting divers' lists.

The impressive Cathedral Cave (Gozo, Site 7) features a huge domed vault.

Comino has several intricate passageways and collapsed caverns, such as Santa Marija Cave (Comino, Site 3), which allow sunlight to penetrate through the water amidst thousands of teeming small fish hand-fed by the passengers on the visiting snorkel boats.

On Gozo a number of caves and caverns are to be found in the Dwejra area (Gozo, sites 10-14). When conditions are perfect at the Inland Sea there is a superb cavern dive through a headland to deep blue water beyond. Directly in front of the Azure Window, nestling at the bottom of Dwejra Point, is the Blue Hole. This natural rock formation, carved out over the centuries by the wind and waves, features a huge arch with a large cave at the bottom. The best cavern in the Dwejra region is the Coral Cave, a giant semi-circular opening with a sandy bottom inside and a tumble of boulders under the entrance. However, the most recent diving fatalities occurred in this cavern, so great care should be taken at all times.

One of Gozo's most popular caves is the Blue Dome (Site 7) at the entrance to the Ghasri Valley. An entrance only 5m (17ft) below the surface leads you through to a huge domed vault, where you can surface and take a breather. The seabed in the cave's interior is covered in massive boulders, while the view to the deep blue of the ocean outside is superb. Nearby is Billinghurst Cave (Site 6), suitable only for experienced cave divers. There is very little natural light penetration here, and the cave dips in the middle, further cutting off daylight.

TRAINING

Caves extending for hundreds of metres underground present a serious undertaking. Divers should never explore beyond the safe limits of the outer caverns without qualified guides or proper training: remember that cave and cavern diving is a specialized skill. As yet only one registered dive centre offers a PADI qualification in this aspect of the sport.

The course consists of over 12 hours of lectures and a minimum of 4 cave dives with double tanks. It helps you to develop a safe working knowledge of the cave environment and covers the following topics: accident analysis; stress management; psychological aspects; dive planning; air management; guidelines and reels; guideline techniques and protocol; equipment configuration; emergency

Many caverns are deep and specialist training is necessary before diving them.

procedures; decompression theory and procedures; landowner relations; team management; and the use of oxygen. The course is run by Aquaventure, Mellhieha Bay Hotel, tel (356) 21522141/fax (356) 21521053; e-mail info@aquaventuremalta.com.

The Marine Environment

THE ROCKY SHORES OF MALTA, COMINO AND GOZO

The Maltese islands are primarily composed of an ancient limestone reef situated on top of an extinct submarine volcanic plateau, which extends to and includes the island of Sicily to the north. The limestone is riddled with underground caves and caverns and features some of the world's most spectacular natural underwater arches. The only rivers are those formed by rainwater run-off, which can cause temporary flooding and reduce the underwater visibility in several gorges such as the Ghasri Valley and Xlendi Bay on Gozo to almost nil, although this bad visibility never lasts for long. Light rain tends to percolate instead down through the porous limestone to the sub-island water table, from where it makes its way to the sea. Consequently, much of the coastline and offshore islands are surrounded by relatively clear water all year round.

The littoral and sublittoral region can be divided into different areas. At the shoreline is an ancient ironstone reef, in most cases very hard, with sharp ridges and water-eroded salt pools created by constant battering from the tide and weather as well as from humans. Much of the shoreline is ancient fossilized seabed, with the remains of sand dollars, molluscs and crinoids in plain view. There are even fossilized dinosaur tracks in several locations.

In lower-lying areas, principally in the north of the islands, the shoreline then extends underwater to form gentle rolling rocky meadows covered in many species of marine algae. In the open sand areas you will find patches of neptune grass (*Posidonia oceanica*) [*Alka* in Malti], the major breeding area for many fish and invertebrate species.

In the southwest of both Gozo and Malta, towering cliffs extend an equal distance underwater, which makes diving akin to diving the wall or drop-off of more tropical oceans. These vertical and underhanging walls are spectacular, allowing for easy exploration at any depth. Many of the walls drop beyond the safe sport diving depth, so care should always be taken with weight and buoyancy control.

MEDITERRANEAN REEFS

The islands' reefs mostly consist of vertical rocky walls, massive eroded caves and caverns, and a substrate of enormous boulders that have tumbled down from the high cliffs above. While not true coral reefs, they are still home to fragile living communities made up of many thousands of individuals, including cnidarians or coral-like animals.

Cnidarians come in many different shapes and sizes, ranging from bright sea fans to sheets of golden colour. The most obvious ones around the islands are soft corals, cup corals and zoanthids. Cup corals such as *Astroides* are tiny, knobby corals that grow singly or in large colonies, and may be found in shaded areas underneath boulders and inside the mouths of caves and caverns.

There are also gorgonian sea fans, coming in a few different varieties, though most are found only in deep water, well offshore, often attaching themselves to deeper wrecks. The yellow sea fan (*Eunicella cavolinii*) and the red sea fan (*Paramuricea clavata*) may be found. The soft coral often known as dead men's fingers (*Alcyonium palmatum*) is also red in colour, with white feeding polyps. Be careful when approaching these animals; they bend in the current and it is easy to misjudge your distance and bump into them. Fan corals are also home to a vast number of invertebrates such as nudibranchs, shrimps and hermit crabs.

Some of the most delicate organisms found here are crustose algae such as the sea rose (*Pseudolithophyllum expansum*), which forms expanding rings of purple in shaded areas such as cave walls and roofs, or on vertical cliff walls. Close by you will find clusters of the sea lace bryozoan (*Reteporella septentrionalis*) as well as branches of the false corals *Porella cervicornis* and *Myriapora truncata*. These can be dislodged easily by your air bubbles as you enter caves, so try to limit such excursions to a minimum. (Fortunately the limestone caverns are porous and much trapped air eventually filters through.) Sponges are also one of the largest groups of animals.

FISH AND OTHER MARINE LIFE

One creature that it is a delight to find is the seahorse (*Hippocampus ramulosus*). This exotically shaped relative of the pipefish (of which there are several species in Maltese waters) has incredible camouflage techniques. Small pieces of algae become attached to the fleshy protuberances behind its head and down its scaly back, rendering it almost invisible amongst the algae-encrusted limestone rocks and boulders. Preferring calm conditions, they are often found near brackish water where salt and fresh water mix. Valletta Harbour, Mellieha Bay, Marfa Point, Mgarr ix-Xini and the Ghasri Valley are good places to look.

Octopuses can be found wandering the algal forests at night, but don't touch. Continual handling of these highly developed molluscs removes the protective mucous membrane from their skin, potentially leading to infection and death.

Turtles are extremely rare in the Mediterranean, and if you are fortunate enough to encounter one, on no account try to hold onto it. If it is sleeping at night, stay well clear: grabbing hold could give the creature such a shock that it might blunder into a cave and be drowned or seriously damage itself and the marine life around it.

Even comparatively common creatures, such as spiny sea urchins, should be treated with respect. Apart from the obvious danger of getting spines embedded in your flesh, a real concern is the illegal act of cutting up these creatures to feed other animals on the reef. It must not be forgotten that urchins play an important part in controlling algae.

Opposite: *Paradise Bay (Malta, Site 29) is a paradise for thousands of small fish.*

CONSERVATION IN THE MALTESE ISLANDS

Most fish are slow in their growth patterns. If an area of reef forming the habitat of a particular fish or invertebrate is damaged, the effect on the rest of the reef's population can be catastrophic. Unfortunately, few conservation measures are implemented in these waters, and there are no statutory marine parks. Many dive schools enforce their own conservation policy and their divers voluntarily police the more popular areas, such as Marfa Point on Malta and Dwejra Point on Gozo. However, local fishermen can be distrustful of divers. It has been known for rocks to be thrown into the water to hit divers who come too close to the area they are fishing. (The best policy for divers is not to risk antagonizing local fishermen and stay well clear.)

In any case, care must always be taken – a misplaced fin or equipment console can seriously wound or kill vulnerable marine creatures. It is essential not only to respect the islands' heritage, but to care for the future of its habitats.

Dwejra Natural and Heritage Park – An EU Life project and beyond

Dwejra in Gozo is one of Malta's leading attractions, visited by nearly every tourist to the Maltese Islands as well as locals, who come to enjoy the scenery and clean sea, swim in the Inland Sea or simply walk and enjoy the peace and quiet of the area. In total, Dwejra attracts over a million visitors each year, including thousands of divers who visit its unique diving area, one of the best in the Mediterranean.

Nature Trust (Malta) – one of Malta's oldest and biggest environmental groups – is working as the beneficiary on a Life funded project to conserve the site and turn it into a Heritage Park and Marine Protected Area. Partners in the project include the Malta Environment and Planning Authority and WWF Italy. The Ministry for Gozo and San Lawrenz Local Council are the major stakeholders.

Following a detailed survey of around 8km^2 of land and sea, conservation work started in 2005. This includes restoration of habitats, setting up an Interpretation centre and providing facilities for visitors. The Park will provide educational facilities, information panels, and guided walks. Finally, the project aims to create management structures for the site, for three main reasons: to save it from further degradation; to conserve the site for future generations to enjoy; and to attain the status of a UNESCO World Heritage Site, EU Natura 2000 Site and a Marine Protected Area. E-mail info@naturetrustmalta.org.

COMMON INVERTEBRATES

The Maltese island chain, because of its central location in the Mediterranean, is particularly rich in marine life and has a high proportion of all the invertebrate species to be found in the region. The following offers a brief description of several of the most common invertebrates. Note that names given in square brackets are local Malti names.

Cnidarians [*Qroll*]

Small Devonshire cup corals (*Caryophyllia smithii*) are found in most shaded areas, but by far the most colourful of all is the golden zoanthid (*Parazoanthus axinellae*), which grows in huge sheets of golden colour under overhangs and at the entrances to many caverns. Smaller individual polyps of golden cup corals (*Astroides calycularis*) can be found in shallower water. Sea fans are rarely seen in shallow water and the yellow sea fan (*Eunicella cavolinii*) is probably the most common on deeper, current-swept reefs.

Crabs [*Granc*] (phylum Crustacea)

Other than hermit crabs, which are commonly found all over Maltese rocky reefs, true crabs such as the spider crab (*Herbstia condyliata*) are considered quite rare. However, their larger relatives, the spiny spider crabs (*Maja squinado* and *Maja crispata*), are seen on virtually every night dive, often covered in an algal fuzz which they cultivate for additional camouflage. The red reef hermit (*Dardanus arrosor*) can be wary of divers.

Fireworm [*Hanex*] (phylum Annelida)

The bearded fireworm (*Hermodice carunculata*) is very common. An active predator, it can grow up to 15cm (6in) and is particularly exotic. The fine hairs or bristles along its body can easily penetrate the skin, and cause a painful irritation.

Sea Urchins [*Rizza*] (phylum Echinodermata)

Sea urchins are very common in all habitats and in all depth ranges. Many can be found at the entry points to dive sites and care should be taken. The most common on rocky substrates is the green sea urchin (*Paracentrotus lividus*), and amongst *Posidonia* you will more commonly find the white-tip sea urchin (*Sphaerechinus granularis*).

Starfish and featherstarfish [*Stilla tal-bahar*] (classes Asteroidea and Crinoidea)

The giant red starfish (*Ophidiaster ophidianus*) often curls itself around golden cup corals. Another large starfish is the common red star (*Echinaster sepositus*), found over beds of algae. Crinoids or featherstarfish (*Antedon mediterranea*) crawl out onto limestone walls as night falls.

CLASSIFICATION AND NOMENCLATURE

The scientific name of an animal is very useful to know. Even when diving in various areas of the same region, you may come across different common names for the same creature, which can lead to confusion. The correct naming of a species (nomenclature) is important for your own logbook records, and is essential to marine biologists studying flora and fauna now and in the future.

The modern binomial system of nomenclature was developed by Linnaeus in his *Systema Naturae*, first published in 1758. The scientific (Latin) name of the animal contains the name of the genus to which it belongs, which always has a capital letter. This is followed by the specific or trivial name, which is always spelt with a small letter, for example *Uranoscopus scaber* (the stargazer), known locally on Malta as *Zondu*.

A number of identification books are available for the amateur marine biologist, some of which are listed in the bibliography.

COMMON FISH

Blenny [*Budakkri*] (families Clinidae, Blennidae, Tripterygiidae)

Few blennies have swim bladders and they tend to perch on corals, hydroids and rubble. Most live in cracks or holes vacated by other marine organisms and defend their territory vigorously. The black-headed blenny (*Tripterygion melanurus*) is quite common and likes cave entrances, although it is very small and difficult to spot.

Triplefin blenny (*Tripterygion xanthosoma*)

Bream [*Sargu*] (family Nemipteridae)

Sea bream are the largest of the species groups to be found in this region. The most common close to shore are the saddled bream (*Oblada melanura*) [*Kahlija*] and the two-banded bream (*Diplodus vulgaris*) [*Xirghien*]. Other members of this large family are pandora (*Pagellus erythrinus*) [*Pagella*], dentex (*Dentex dentex*) [*Denci*] and salema (*Sarpa salpa*) [*Xilpa*], which are unpopular with fishermen and can therefore be found in huge shoals all around the coast.

Two-banded bream (*Diplodus vulgaris*)

Cardinalfish [*Sultan ic-cawl*] (family Apogonidae)

Cardinalfish (*Apogon imberbis*) are very common around the Maltese islands and can be found on virtually every dive where there is a rocky substrate, ranging from offshore reefs to vertical walls. They like small recesses and live together in little groups. Very approachable, they usually make excellent photographic subjects.

Cardinalfish (*Apogon imberbis*)

Goatfish/Mullet [*Trilja*] (family Mullidae)

There are two species of goatfish found around the islands: *Mullus barbatus* [*Trilja bla faxxi*], which is mottled in colour with a flat squarish head, and the more common striped red mullet (*Mullus surmeletus*) [*Trilja tal-faxxi*], which when feeding can be found in small groups foraging in the sand with their specially adapted pectoral fins. These whisker-like barbels are used like fingers to search for small crustaceans and worms.

Red mullet (*Mullus surmeletus*)

Gobies [*Mzazen*] (family Gobiidae)

Gobies are small fish and, like many blennies, do not possess a swim bladder; consequently they swim only in short bursts. They differ from blennies in having two or three separate dorsal fins (blennies, by contrast, have a continuous dorsal fin from the back of the head to the tail). Bucchichi's goby (*Gobius bucchichii*) [*Mazzun kanella*] is generally found only on sand and along the edges of *Posidonia* beds.

Bucchichi's goby (*Gobius bucchichii*)

Parrotfish (*Sparisoma cretense*)

Parrotfish [*Marzpan*] (*family Scaridae*)
The only parrotfish species in the Mediterranean (*Sparisoma cretense*) is small and brightly coloured, with a dark red body and blue-grey patch with a yellow bar behind the head and a yellow patch on the back, just before its tail. Parrotfish are born as hermaphrodites, then turn into females; some eventually attain a supermale size. They move around in small feeding packs. The supermale grows to 32cm (13in) and is a dull grey-brown colour.

Red scorpionfish (*Scorpaena notata*)

Scorpionfish [*Skorfna*] (*family Scorpaenidae*)
Three species of scorpionfish are found around the Maltese islands. The most common species is the small red scorpionfish (*Scorpaena notata*) [*Skorfna tattebgha*]. Scorpionfish are most often seen at night, when divers' torches happen to pick up the brightly coloured pectoral fins as the fish move off rapidly after being disturbed.

Seahorse (*Hippocampus ramulosus*)

Seahorses [*Ziemel*] (*family Hippocampinae*)
Two species of seahorse are found around the Maltese islands, the rarer and smaller *Hippocampus hippocampus* [*Ziemel tal-bahar halqa qasir*], which has a short snout and no crest-like appendages, and *Hippocampus ramulosus* [*Ziemel tal-bahar halqa twil*], which features a long snout and a crest that extends from its head to its dorsal fin.

Picarel (*Spicara smaris*)

Silverfish (*families Atherinidae, Clupeidae, Engraulididae*)
The smallest of the silverfish most likely to attract your attention are sardines (*Sardinella aurita*) [*Lacca*]. These small fish grow up to only 8cm (3in) and are often seen with bogue (*Boops boops*) [*Vopa*], anchovy (*Engraulis encrasicolus*) [*Incova*] and picarel (*Spicara smaris*) [*Arznell*]. During their juvenile stage they are vulnerable and group together in huge shoals amongst the gulleys and caves close to the shore.

Snouted wrasse (*Symphodus doderleini*)

Wrasse [*Tirda*] (*family Labridae*)
The most common is the snouted wrasse (*Symphodus doderleini*) [*Tirda tar-rig abjad*]. It grows up to 20cm (8in) and has a long snout, protruding lips, and a cream and brown band in front of the eye. The most common of the smaller species is the green wrasse (*Labrus viridis*) [*Tirda*], while the cuckoo wrasse (*Labrus bimaculatus*) [*Parpanjol*] is by far the most colourful. Both species go through several colour changes before reaching maturity.

Underwater Photography and Video

For those who want to record their dives accurately, then underwater photography is the answer. From my earliest days of diving, I struggled to remember every detail of a dive or to be able to describe the intricacies of the colour markings on a species of fish to try and identify it properly. In fact, there were very few identification books available at the time. In the past 35 years, however, all that has changed dramatically. The world's first amphibious camera for the mass market was designed by Jean de Wouters d'Oplinter and developed by Jacques-Yves Cousteau. From there, the industry has evolved to making specialized lenses, flash and waterproof housings to fit the world's most advanced camera systems and technology.

EQUIPMENT

For the beginner, perhaps the best way to start is with an instant disposable camera. These are inexpensive and give immediate results. However, such cameras are usually good only to about 2m (6ft) of depth. An alternative is to rent a waterproof box which allows you to use your land camera down to 30m (100ft). Submersible waterproof housings can be bulky, but they are strong, reliable and are cheaper than the last and most sophisticated option, a dedicated underwater camera such as the Nikonos RS-AF.

To take photographs underwater, you must think not only of the camera. As your ability progresses, your camera needs to be compatible with as great a variety of equipment as possible. This will include a choice of lenses, a flash and the means to connect it to the camera. Lighting underwater is always with a waterproof flash of some type and this needs to be compatible with whichever camera or housing you choose. If you are unsure of which system to buy, then a sensible option is to rent an outfit from one or other of the principal dive centres on Malta or Gozo, and perhaps also attend an instruction course to learn about the intricacies of each type.

No matter what type of system you choose, whether it be the amphibious type such as the Nikonos RS-AF or Sea & Sea system, or an SLR camera housed in a waterproof box, you must always treat it with the greatest respect and care. Before any trip, ensure that all of the connections are clean and that all 'O' rings are free of dust and are given a light coat of silicone grease. Also check for any nicks or cuts in the seals. Ensure that the flash fires correctly with the camera shutter and that you have sufficient power to operate. For those with rechargeable flash, make certain that the recharger works and that it is compatible with the electrical supply on the islands (240 volts, using square three-pin plugs as in the UK; 110 volts also available through hotel shaver sockets).

The best film for underwater use is generally of the slide or transparency variety with film speeds of between 50 and 100 ISO. This allows for better sharpness and colour reproduction. For instant cameras, print film with a film speed between 200 and 400 ISO is more common. This faster film is also much more suited to the low-light conditions experienced in caves and caverns.

WIDE-ANGLE PHOTOGRAPHY

Wide angle is by far the most popular form of underwater photography. A wide-angle lens will allow you to take perspective photographs of, for example, the deeper caves and caverns off Dwejra Point, the Azure Window or Inland Sea, or on any of the wrecks in the Valletta area. To see a diver surrounded by bright marine life with a deep blue background gives a wonderful feel for the scene you are viewing. Wide-angle photographs are also the most published by magazines, and this type of lens is the preferred choice of many professional underwater photographers.

DIGITAL PHOTOGRAPHY

Digital photography is the most easily accessible and usable form of underwater photography today. More people buy digital cameras than any other type and many manufacturers produce bespoke waterproof housings for different models. The standard 'point and shoot' type are easiest to use and when on 'auto' or 'macro' settings produce instant gratification, as you are able to view the image immediately underwater, download the pictures onto a computer and email them to your envious friends!

There are obviously more advanced, professional digital cameras that act exactly like the older style single lens reflex cameras, where you can choose the aperture, shutter speed, equivalent film speed and compose your

WIDE-ANGLE APPLICATIONS

- Cliff and reef drop-off panoramas
- Exteriors of shipwrecks
- Interiors of shipwrecks and caves
- Divers in action
- Divers and fish/animal interaction
- Large fish
- Available light and silhouettes
- Wide-angle flash and flash-fill techniques

BENEFITS OF MACRO PHOTOGRAPHY

- A different perspective
- High magnification
- Maximum colour saturation
- Sharp focus
- Ease of learning and execution
- Can be done anywhere, under almost any conditions
- Easiest to use on night dives
- Greatest return for the least investment

---

subject matter 'through the lens'. Judging by the standard of photographs being produced digitally, the format is here to stay and will, for many people, mean the demise of 35mm film use underwater.

MACRO PHOTOGRAPHY

Macro photography is a form of underwater photography where the camera lens is positioned very close to a subject to record a relatively large image on film and produce an image of high magnification of the subject. I recommend that you start underwater photography with a macro system, as it is undoubtedly the easiest form of underwater photography. The frustrations common to many other types of photography are minimized and very soon you will be amazed by the sharp images and vibrant colours that only macro photography can produce.

The different perspective that macro photography gives opens up a whole new world of tiny animals and plants not normally seen during average diving conditions. Your eyes quickly learn to find creatures small enough to fit the format and, as a result, what were once boring dives on gravel beds or sandy bottoms or under jetties suddenly start to yield a wealth of life.

A BEGINNERS' GUIDE TO TAKING SUCCESSSFUL UNDERWATER PHOTOGRAPHS

With macro photography it seems as if you can become an expert overnight, but the pursuit of underwater images is a life-long experience. Allow time to learn about composition, and you will find your technique steadily improves.

Prior to taking up underwater photography, it is recommended that you attend an underwater photography workshop. There are a number of centres specializing in this type of instruction, and classes are scheduled throughout the year. Even non-photographer 'buddies' will benefit from the classes, since modelling, composition and buoyancy are all important factors in a successful photograph.

- Approach one photographic technique or problem at a time. Do not try to do everything at once.
- Record the technical details of each photograph (aperture, speed, distance etc.) as you take them, to find out which settings get the best results.

- Keep your flash or strobe well away from the camera (unless working in a macro situation). Position it to the top left of the camera so that the light beam makes an angle of 45° along the camera-to-subject axis.
- Pre-aim the flash out of the water to obtain the correct camera-to-subject position. If you need to change the setting underwater, aim the flash one-third behind the apparent position to counter the effects of refraction.
- Find the aperture that produces the most consistent results for you. Next time you take photographs at that setting take an extra photograph, one either side of that aperture (one stop lower and one stop higher). Called 'bracketing', this will take care of subjects with different degrees of brightness.
- Get as close as you can to your subject. Close-ups have the most impact and better colour saturation.
- Note the position of the sun when you enter the water. Use the sun to create back-lit shots to add depth and interest.
- Never take pictures below you; always shoot horizontally or upwards.
- Pre-set your focus and allow the subject and yourself to approach each other slowly and carefully.
- Take your photographs in clear water and bright sunlight if you can.
- Never use the flash when the camera-to-subject distance is greater than one-fifth of the underwater visibility. If the visibility is 5m (16½ft), focus and use the flash at only 1m (3ft), which will cut down the 'back scatter' of particles in suspension in the water.
- Set your camera to the fastest aperture that the flash will synchronize to (unless using an automatic housed system).
- Be ruthless. The only way to learn is by self-criticism, so put as much film through the camera as possible and learn by your mistakes.

FILM AND CAMERA TIPS

- If you have to buy film locally, do so from a top photography outlet or a major hotel, where the turnover of stock will be reasonably swift and where the film will have spent most of its storage life in cool conditions.
- If you keep film refrigerated, give it at least two hours to defrost before putting it in a camera.
- Do not assemble underwater cameras in cool, air-conditioned rooms or cabins. Condensation is likely to form inside them when you take them into the water.
- Normal cameras that have been in an air-conditioned environment will mist up when you take them out into the warm atmosphere. You need to wait at least ten minutes for the condensation to dissipate before you can take clear photographs.
- For digital camera users, always have spare batteries or rechargeable battery packs (specific to your camera) as well as extra memory cards for storing your precious photographs, before downloading to a computer.

Underwater Video

Stills photography is all very well for recording that tiny moment in time of a marine subject. But when you are faced with the prospect of swimming through a hole in the wall surrounded by millions of silversides, then video is what you need. People are transfixed by the moving image and nothing tells the story of the dancing wonders of the reef better. Several dive stores in the Maltese islands have underwater video equipment for rent and by renting you can soon find out for yourself which of the many systems on offer you prefer. The format is changing constantly and it is difficult to keep up with the latest technological developments in underwater video.

EQUIPMENT

Virtually all video cameras available are primarily designed for the terrestrial holiday market, and the sophistication of the waterproof housings which have been developed for them sometimes seems nonsensical. Housings come in a variety of styles and sizes: all have waterproof controls to allow you to use the camera's functions, though some are more awkward to handle than others, especially with lights attached. It is important to choose a system with a good-quality housing, such as those made by Sony, Panasonic and other well known manufacturers. These are readily available by mail order from most diving-related magazines.

The quality of the video image has improved by leaps and bounds in recent years, while in the meantime cameras have become smaller and lighter. One problem with systems now being so light is that with hand-held shots you may get camera shake. Whenever possible, with close-up work or a marine life study, make use of a tripod.

Lighting systems have also undergone a revolution these last few years. Many of the lights fixed on the video housing are very light, and the bulky and heavy battery pack may be extended to a clamp which attaches onto your diving air tank. On a number of other housings, the battery pack is held in a sling under the housing, which helps with the stability of the system.

A basic advantage of video over photography is that there is no waste of film. You can re-use the tape at any time. The only major problem you are likely to come up against with underwater video is rechargeable power packs. You need always to remember to change each pack before you dive and to make sure that you have enough power in store to catch that magic moment that may arise during a dive.

BUOYANCY CONTROL

As an underwater photographer, I am acutely conscious of very occasional moments of accidental contact that I have with the coral reef. All divers MUST master the art of buoyancy control. Apart from the primary need to avoid damaging corals, buoyancy control is an important aspect of taking good underwater photographs and videography.

The basic need is to be able to hover both horizontally and vertically close to the reef or the bottom without a need to actually make contact. Buoyancy is principally controlled by inflating or deflating your buoyancy compensator at various depths. Once expert buoyancy has been achieved, you will notice a drastic reduction in your air consumption, see more marine life on each dive and find your pleasure increase accordingly, as well as, of course, dramatically cutting down on accidental environmental damage.

SHOOTING SEQUENCES

Try and plan your shooting sequences before entering the water and stick to that plan as best you can. Of course, there is always the chance that something totally unexpected will happen and you should be ready for all eventualities. It is best to avoid diving with inexperienced divers or trainees, as they will inevitably get in the way. Train your buddy to help you.

Try not to prolong the sequence that you are filming. Too long a sequence is boring and more difficult to edit. Keep the direction of movement of divers constant and whenever possible have the divers and fish swimming towards the camera. The best situation is for your diving buddy/model to swim to the other side of the reef and then swim towards you. As they approach, the fish in front of the person will automatically swim towards you, making for a more interesting shot. Take occasional cut-away shots – small vignettes of diver portraits, fish behaviour, close-ups of anemone tentacles and so on.

EDITING

Editing your video is fun, but can also be frustrating, as you have to be ruthless with your choice of clips. The difficulty is not what to leave in, but rather what to take out. Your audience will soon get bored if the video is too long and of the same subject matter. Study any of the wildlife films on television and try to emulate them: this is as good a way as any for learning editing technique. Your video will also be greatly enhanced by the addition of sound and commentary – again, try not to get too technical, and perhaps use someone else's voice to add a touch of professionalism.

Health and Safety for Divers

The information on first aid and safety in this part of the book is intended as a guide only. It is based on currently accepted health and safety guidelines, but it is merely a summary and is no substitute for a comprehensive manual on the subject – or, even better, for first aid training. We strongly advise you to buy a recognized manual on diving safety and medicine before setting off on a diving trip, to read it through during the journey, and to carry it with you to refer to during the trip. It would also be sensible to take a short course in first aid.

We urge anyone in need of advice on emergency treatment to see a doctor as soon as possible.

WHAT TO DO IN AN EMERGENCY
- Divers who have suffered any injury or symptom of an injury, no matter how minor, related to diving, should consult a doctor, preferably a specialist in diving medicine, as soon as possible after the symptom or injury occurs.
- No matter how confident you are in making a diagnosis, remember that you are an amateur diver and an unqualified medical practitioner.
- If you are the victim of a diving injury do not let fear of ridicule prevent you from revealing your symptoms. Apparently minor symptoms can mask or even develop into a life-threatening illness. It is better to be honest with yourself and live to dive another day.
- Always err on the conservative side when treating an illness or an injury. If you find that the condition is only minor you – and the doctor – will both be relieved.

FIRST AID
The basic principles of first aid are to:
- do no harm
- sustain life
- prevent deterioration
- promote recovery.

If you have to treat an ill or injured person:
- First try to secure the safety of yourself and the ill or injured person by getting the two of you out of the threatening environment: the water.
- Think before you act: do not do anything that will further endanger either of you.
- Then follow a simple sequence of patient assessment and management:
  1 Assess whether you are dealing with a life-threatening condition.
  2 If so, try to define which one.
  3 Then try to manage the condition.

Assessing the ABCs:
Learn the basic checks – the ABCs:
A: for AIRWAY (with care of the neck)
B : for BREATHING
C: for CIRCULATION
D: for DECREASED level of consciousness
E: for EXPOSURE (a patient must be exposed enough for a proper examination to be made).

- **Airway (with attention to the neck):** check whether the patient has a neck injury. Are the mouth and nose free from obstruction? Noisy breathing is a sign of airway obstruction.

- **Breathing:** look at the chest to see if it is rising and falling. Listen for air movement at the nose and mouth. Feel for the movement of air against your cheek.

- **Circulation:** feel for a pulse (the carotid artery) next to the windpipe.

- **Decreased level of consciousness:** does the patient respond in any of the following ways?
    A - Awake, aware, spontaneous speech.
    V - Verbal Stimuli: does he or she answer to 'Wake up?'
    P - Painful Stimuli: does he or she respond to a pinch?
    U - Unresponsive.

- **Exposure:** preserve the dignity of the patient as much as you can, but remove clothes as necessary to carry out your treatment.

Now, send for help
If, after your assessment, you think the condition of the patient is serious, you must send or call for help from the nearest emergency services (ambulance, paramedics). Tell whoever you send for help to come back and let you know whether help is on the way.

Recovery position
If the patient is unconscious but breathing normally there is a risk that he or she may vomit and choke on the vomit. It is therefore critical that the patient be turned on one side with arms outstretched in front of the body. This is called the recovery position and it is illustrated in all first aid manuals.

If you suspect injury to the spine or neck, immobilize the patient in a straight line before you turn him or her on one side.

If the patient is unconscious, does not seem to be breathing, and you cannot feel a pulse, do not try to turn him or her into the recovery position.

If you cannot feel a pulse

If your patient has no pulse you will have to carry out CPR (Cardiopulmonary Resuscitation). This consists of techniques to:

- ventilate the patient's lungs (expired air resuscitation)
- pump the patient's heart (external cardiac compression).

CPR (Cardiopulmonary Resuscitation)

Airway

Open the patient's airway by gently extending the head (head tilt) and lifting the chin with two fingers (chin lift). This lifts the patient's tongue away from the back of the throat and opens the airway. If the patient is unconscious and you think something may be blocking the airway, sweep your finger across the back of the tongue from one side to the other. If you find anything, remove it. Do not try this if the patient is conscious or semi-conscious because he or she may bite your finger or vomit.

Breathing: EAR (Expired Air Resuscitation)

If the patient is not breathing you need to give the 'kiss of life', or expired air resuscitation (EAR) – you breathe into his or her lungs. The 16 per cent of oxygen in the air you expire is enough to keep your patient alive.

1 Pinch the patient's nose to close the nostrils.
2 Place your open mouth fully over the patient's mouth, making as good a seal as possible.
3 Exhale into the patient's mouth hard enough to make the chest rise and fall. Give two long slow breaths.
4 If the patient's chest fails to rise, try adjusting the position of the airway.
5 Check the patient's pulse. If you cannot feel one, follow the instructions under 'Circulation' below. If you can, continue breathing for the patient once every five seconds, checking the pulse after every ten breaths.
- If the patient begins breathing, turn him or her into the recovery position (see page 103).

Circulation

If, after giving expired air resuscitation, you cannot feel a pulse, you should try external cardiac compression:

1 Kneel next to the patient's chest.
2 Measure two finger breadths above the notch where the ribs meet the lower end of the breast bone.
3 Place the heel of your left hand just above your two fingers in the centre of the breast bone.
4 Place the heel of your right hand on your left hand.
5 Straighten your elbows.
6 Place your shoulders perpendicularly above the patient's breast bone.
7 Compress the breast bone 4–5cm (1½–2in) to a rhythm of 'one, two, three . . .'
8 Carry out 15 compressions.

Continue giving cycles of 2 breaths and 15 compressions, checking for a pulse after every 5 cycles. The aim of CPR

is to keep the patient alive until paramedics or a doctor arrive with the necessary equipment.

Check before you dive that you and your buddy are both trained in CPR. If not, get some training – it could mean the difference between life and death for either of you or for someone else.

DIVING DISEASES AND ILLNESSES

Acute decompression illness

Acute decompression illness is any illness arising from the decompression of a diver – in other words, by the diver moving from an area of high ambient pressure to an area of low pressure. There are two types of acute decompression illness:

- decompression sickness ('the bends')
- barotrauma with arterial gas embolism.

ROUGH AND READY NONSPECIALIST TESTS FOR THE BENDS

If you suspect a diver may be suffering from the bends, carry out these tests. If the results of your checks do not seem normal, the diver may be suffering from the bends and you must take emergency action. Take the appropriate action outlined on page 104 even if you are not sure of your assessment – the bends is a life-threatening illness.

1 Does the diver know:
   who he/she is?
   where he/she is?
   what the time is?
2 Can the diver see and count the number of fingers you hold up? Hold your hand 50cm (20in) in front of the diver's face and ask him/her to follow your hand with his/her eyes as you move it from side to side and up and down. Be sure that both eyes follow in each direction, and look out for any rapid oscillation or jerky movements of the eyeballs.
3 Ask the diver to smile, and check that both sides of the face have the same expression. Run the back of a finger across each side of the diver's forehead, cheeks and chin, and ask whether he/she can feel it.
4 Check that the diver can hear you whisper when his/her eyes are closed.
5 Ask the diver to shrug his/her shoulders. Both should move equally.
6 Ask the diver to swallow. Check that the adam's apple moves up and down.
7 Ask the diver to stick out his/her tongue at the centre of the mouth – deviation to either side indicates a problem.
8 Check the diver has equal muscle strength on both sides of the body. You do this by pulling/pushing each of the diver's arms and legs away from and back toward the body, asking him/her to resist you.
9 Run your finger lightly across the diver's shoulders, down the back, across the chest and abdomen, and along the arms and legs, feeling upper and underside surfaces. Check that the diver can feel your finger moving along each surface.
10 On firm ground (not on a boat) check that the diver can walk in a straight line and, with eyes closed, stand upright with feet together and arms outstretched.

It is not important for the diver or first aider to be able to differentiate between the bends and barotrauma because both are serious, life-threatening illnesses, and both require the same emergency treatment. The important thing is to be able to recognize acute decompression illness and to initiate emergency treatment. The list below and the box on page 103 outline the signs and symptoms to look out for.

The bends (decompression sickness)

Decompression sickness or 'the bends' occurs when a diver has not been adequately decompressed. Exposure to higher ambient pressure underwater causes nitrogen to dissolve in increasing amounts in the body tissues. If this pressure is released gradually during correct and adequate decompression procedures, the nitrogen escapes naturally into the blood and is exhaled through the lungs. If the release of pressure is too rapid, the nitrogen cannot escape quickly enough and bubbles of nitrogen gas form in the tissues. The symptoms and signs of the disease are related to the tissues in which the bubbles form, and it is described by the tissues affected – joint bend, for example.

Symptoms and signs include:
- nausea and vomiting
- dizziness
- malaise
- weakness
- pains in the joints
- paralysis
- numbness
- itching of skin
- incontinence.

Barotrauma with arterial gas embolism

Barotrauma is the damage that occurs when the tissue surrounding a gaseous space is injured following a change in the volume of air in that space. An arterial gas embolism is a gas bubble that moves in a blood vessel; this usually leads to the obstruction of that blood vessel or a vessel further downstream.

Barotrauma can occur in any tissue surrounding a gas-filled space. Common sites and types of barotrauma are:
- ears (middle ear squeeze) → burst ear drum
- sinuses (sinus squeeze) → sinus pain/nose bleeds
- lungs (lung squeeze) → burst lung
- face (mask squeeze) → swollen, bloodshot eyes
- teeth (tooth squeeze) → toothache.

Burst lung is the most serious of these since it can result in arterial gas embolism. It occurs following a rapid ascent during which the diver does not exhale adequately. The rising pressure of expanding air in the lungs bursts the delicate alveoli – air sacs in the lungs – and forces air into the blood vessels that carry blood back to the heart and, ultimately, the brain. In the brain these air bubbles block blood vessels and obstruct the supply of blood and oxygen to the brain. This causes brain damage.

The symptoms and signs of lung barotrauma and arterial gas embolism include:
- shortness of breath
- chest pain
- unconsciousness.

Treatment of acute decompression Illness:
- ABCs and CPR (see pages 102-3) as necessary
- position the patient in the recovery position (see page 102) with no tilt or raising of the legs
- give 100 per cent oxygen by mask or demand valve
- keep the patient warm
- remove to the nearest hospital as soon as possible. The hospital or emergency services will arrange for recompression treatment.

Carbon dioxide or carbon monoxide poisoning

Carbon dioxide poisoning can occur as a result of skip breathing (diver holds breath on SCUBA), heavy exercise on SCUBA or malfunctioning rebreather systems. Carbon monoxide poisoning occurs as a result of: exhaust gases being pumped into cylinders; hookah systems; air intake too close to exhaust fumes.

Symptoms and signs of carbon monoxide poisoning:
- blue colour of the skin
- shortness of breath
- loss of consciousness.

Treatment of carbon monoxide poisoning:
- get the patient to a safe environment
- ABCs and CPR (see pages 102-3) as necessary
- 100 per cent oxygen through a mask or demand valve
- get the patient to hospital.

Head injury

Any head injury should be treated as serious.

Treatment of a head injury:
- the diver must surface and do no more diving until a doctor has been consulted
- disinfect the wound
- if the diver is unconscious, contact the emergency services
- if breathing and/or pulse have stopped, administer CPR (see page 103)
- if the diver is breathing and has a pulse, check for bleeding and other injuries, and treat for shock
- if the wounds permit, put the injured person into the recovery position and, if possible, give 100 per cent oxygen
- keep the patient warm and comfortable and monitor pulse and respiration constantly.

Do **NOT** give fluids to unconscious or semi-conscious divers.

Hyperthermia (raised body temperature)

A rise in body temperature results from a combination of overheating, normally due to exercise, and inadequate fluid intake. A person with hyperthermia will progress through heat exhaustion to heat stroke, with eventual collapse. Heat stroke is an emergency: if the diver is not cooled and rehydrated he or she will die.

Treatment of hyperthermia:
- move the diver as quickly as possible into a cooler place and remove all clothes
- call the emergency services
- sponge the diver's body with a damp cloth and fan him or her manually or with an electric fan
- if the patient is unconscious, put him or her into the recovery position (see page 102) and monitor the ABCs as necessary
- if the patient is conscious you can give him or her a cold drink.

Hypothermia (low body temperature)

Normal internal body temperature is just under 37°C (98.4°F). If for any reason it falls much below this – usually, in diving, because of inadequate protective clothing – progressively more serious symptoms may follow, and the person will eventually die if the condition is not treated rapidly. A drop of 1C° (2F°) causes shivering and discomfort. A 2C° (3F°) drop induces the body's self-heating mechanisms to react: blood flow to the hands and feet is reduced and shivering becomes extreme. A 3C° (5F°) drop results in memory loss, confusion, disorientation, irregular heartbeat and breathing.and eventually death.

Treatment of hypothermia:
- move the diver as quickly as possible into a sheltered and warm place; *or:*
- prevent further heat loss: use an exposure bag; surround the diver with buddies' bodies; cover his or her head and neck with a woolly hat, warm towels or anything else suitable
- if you have managed to get the diver into sheltered warmth, remove wet clothing, dress your patient in warm, dry clothing and wrap him or her in an exposure bag or heat blanket; however, if you are still in the open, the diver is best left in existing garments
- if the diver is conscious and coherent administer a warm shower or bath and a warm, sweet drink
- if the diver is unconscious, check the ABCs (see page 102), call the emergency services, make the patient as warm as possible, and treat for shock (see page 106).

Near-drowning

Near-drowning is a medical condition in which a diver has inhaled some water – water in the lungs interferes with the normal transport of oxygen from the lungs into the bloodstream. A person in a near-drowning condition may be conscious or unconscious.

Near-drowning victims sometimes develop secondary drowning, a condition in which fluid oozing into the lungs causes the diver to drown in internal secretions, so all near-drowning patients must be monitored in a hospital.

Treatment of near-drowning:
- get the diver out of the water and check the ABCs (see page 102); depending on your findings, begin EAR or CPR (see page 103) as appropriate
- if possible, administer oxygen by mask or demand valve
- call the emergency services and get the diver to a hospital for observation, even if he/she appears to have recovered from the experience.

Nitrogen narcosis

Air contains about 80 per cent nitrogen. Breathing the standard diving mixture under compression can lead to symptoms very much like those of drunkenness (nitrogen narcosis is popularly known as 'rapture of the deep'). Some divers experience nitrogen narcosis at depths of 30–40m (100–130ft). Down to a depth of about 60m (200ft) – which is beyond the legal maximum depth for sport-diving in the UK and the USA – the symptoms are not always serious; but below about 80m (260ft) a diver is likely to lose consciousness. Symptoms can occur very suddenly. Nitrogen narcosis is not a serious condition, but a diver suffering from it may do something dangerous.

Treatment of nitrogen narcosis: the only treatment for this condition is to get the diver to ascend immediately to shallower waters.

TRAVELLING MEDICINE

Many doctors decline to issue drugs, particularly antibiotics, to people who want them 'just in case'; but a diving holiday can be ruined by an ear or sinus infection, especially in a remote area or on a live-aboard boat, where the nearest doctor or pharmacy is a long and difficult journey away.

Many travelling divers therefore carry with them medical kits that could lead the uninitiated to think they are hypochondriacs. Nasal sprays, ear drops, antihistamine creams, anti-diarrhoea medicines, antibiotics, sea-sickness remedies . . . Forearmed, such divers can take immediate action as soon as they realize something is wrong. At the very least, this may minimize their loss of diving time.

Always bear in mind that most decongestants and remedies for sea-sickness can make you drowsy and therefore should NEVER be taken before diving.

Shock

Shock is a medical condition and not just the emotional trauma of a frightening experience. Medical shock results from poor blood and oxygen delivery to the tissues. As a result of oxygen and blood deprivation the tissues cannot carry out their functions. There are many causes; the most common is loss of blood.

Treatment for medical shock:
This is directed at restoring blood and oxygen delivery to the tissues:

- check the ABCs (see page 102)
- give 100 per cent oxygen
- control any external bleeding by pressing hard on the wound and/or pressure points (the location of the pressure points is illustrated in first-aid manuals); raise the injured limb or other part of the body
- use a tourniquet only as a last resort and only on the arms and legs
- if the diver is conscious, lay him/her on the back with the legs raised and the head to one side; if unconscious, turn him or her on the left side in the recovery position (see page 102).

MARINE-RELATED AILMENTS

Sunburn, coral cuts, swimmers' ear, sea-sickness and bites from various insects are perhaps the most common divers' complaints – but there are more serious marine-related illnesses you should know about.

Cuts and abrasions

Divers should wear appropriate abrasive protection for the undersea environment. Hands, knees, elbows and feet are the areas most commonly affected. The danger with abrasions is that they become infected, so all wounds must be thoroughly washed and rinsed with water and an antiseptic as soon as possible after the injury. Infection may progress to a stage where antibiotics are necessary. If the site of an apparently minor injury becomes inflamed, and the inflammation spreads, consult a doctor immediately – you may need antibiotics to prevent the infection spreading to the bloodstream.

Swimmers' ear

Swimmers' ear is an infection of the external ear canal caused by constantly wet ears. The condition is often a combined fungal and bacterial infection. To prevent it, always dry your ears thoroughly after diving. If you know you are susceptible to the condition, insert alcohol drops after diving. If an infection occurs, the best treatment is to stop diving or swimming for a few days and apply ear drops such as:

- 5 per cent acetic acid in isopropyl alcohol; *or*
- aluminium acetate/acetic acid solution.

FIRST-AID KIT

Your first-aid kit should be waterproof, compartmentalized and sealable, and, as a minimum, should contain the following items:

- a full first-aid manual – the information in this appendix is for general guidance only
- contact numbers for the emergency services
- coins for telephone
- pencil and notebook
- tweezers
- scissors
- 6 large standard sterile dressings
- 1 large Elastoplast/Band-Aid fabric dressing strip
- 2 triangular bandages
- 3 medium-size safety pins
- 1 pack sterile cotton wool
- 2 50mm (2in) crepe bandages
- eyedrops
- antiseptic fluid/cream
- bottle of vinegar
- sachets of rehydration salts
- sea-sickness tablets
- decongestants
- painkillers
- anti-AIDS pack (syringes/needles/drip needle)

Sea or motion sickness

Motion sickness can be an annoying complication on a diving holiday involving boat dives. If you suffer from motion sickness, discuss the problem with a doctor before your holiday – or at least before boarding the boat. But bear in mind that many medicines formulated to prevent travel sickness contain antihistamines, which make you drowsy and will impair your ability to think quickly while you are diving.

Biting insects

Some regions are notorious for biting insects. Take a good insect repellent and some antihistamine cream to relieve the effects.

Sunburn

Be sure to take plenty of precautions against sunburn, which can cause skin cancer. Many people get sunburned on the first day of a holiday and spend a very uncomfortable time afterwards recovering. Pay particular attention to the head, the nose and the backs of the legs. Always use high-protection factor creams, and wear clothes that keep off the sun.

Tropical diseases

Visit the doctor before your trip and make sure you have the appropriate vaccinations for the regions you intend to visit on your trip.

Fish that bite

- **Barracuda** These very rarely bite divers, although they have been known to bite in turbid or murky, shallow water, where sunlight flashing on a knife blade, a camera lens or jewellery has confused the fish into thinking they are attacking their normal prey.

  Treatment: clean the wounds thoroughly and use anti-septic or antibiotic cream. Bad bites will also need antibiotic and anti-tetanus treatment.

- **Moray eels** Probably more divers are bitten by morays than by all other sea creatures added together – usually through putting their hands into holes to collect shells or lobsters, remove anchors, or hide baitfish. Once it bites, a moray often refuses to let go, so you may have to persuade it to by gripping it behind the head and exerting pressure with your finger and thumb until it opens its jaw. You can make the wound worse by tearing your flesh if you pull the fish off.

  Treatment: thorough cleaning and usually stitching. The bites always go septic, so have antibiotics and anti-tetanus available.

- **Sharks** Sharks rarely attack divers, but should always be treated with great respect. Their attacks are usually connected with speared or hooked fish, fish or meat set up as bait, lobsters rattling when picked up, or certain types of vibration, such as that produced by helicopters. The decomposition products of dead fish (even several days old) seem much more attractive to most sharks than fresh blood. The main exception is the great white shark, whose normal prey is the sea lion or seal, and which may mistake a diver for one of these. You are very unlikely to see a great white shark. Other sharks often give warning by bumping into you first. If you are frightened, a shark will detect this from the vibrations given off by your body. Calmly back up to the reef or boat and get out of the water.

  Treatment: a person who has been bitten by a shark usually has severe injuries and is suffering from shock. If possible, stop any bleeding by applying pressure. The patient will need to be stabilized with blood or plasma transfusions, so call an ambulance or get the diver to hospital. Even minor wounds are likely to become infected, so the diver will need antibiotic and anti-tetanus treatment.

- **Triggerfish** Large triggerfish – usually males guarding eggs in 'nests' – are particularly aggressive and will attack divers who get too close. Their teeth are very strong, and can go through rubber fins and draw blood through a 4mm (1/6in) wet suit.

  Treatment: clean the wound and treat it with anti-septic cream.

Venomous sea creatures

Many venomous sea creatures are bottom-dwellers – they hide among coral or rest on or burrow into sand. If you need to move along the sea bottom, shuffle along, so that you push such creatures out of the way and minimize the risk of stepping directly onto sharp venomous spines, many of which can pierce rubber fins. Antivenins require specialist medical supervision, do not work for all species, and need refrigerated storage, so they are rarely available when they are needed. Most of the venoms are proteins of high molecular weight that break down under heat.

General treatment: tie a broad bandage at a point between the limb and the body and tighten it. Remember to release it every 15 minutes. Immerse the limb in hot water (perhaps the cooling water from an outboard motor if no other supply is available) at 50°C (120°F) for two hours, until the pain stops. Several injections around the wound of local anaesthetic (such as procaine hydrochloride), if available, will ease the pain. Young or weak people may need CPR (see page 103). Remember that venoms may still be active in fish that have been dead for 48 hours.

- **Fireworms** These small worms with clumps of white hairs along their sides display bristles when touched. The bristles easily break off on the skin, causing a painful burning feeling and intense irritation.

  Treatment: treat affected area with hot water and acetic acid (vinegar).

- **Jellyfish** Most jellyfish sting, but few are dangerous. When seasonal changes are in their favour you may encounter the by-the-wind sailor (*Velella velella*), which can be highly toxic. Continued exposure to the stinging cells may require hospital treatment. The common jellyfish (*Aurelia aurita*) is not dangerous, but the fine tentacles around the perimeter of the bell can sting softer tissue parts such as your neck, face, inner thighs and arms. At night, many of these stingers are almost invisible in the water column and you are advised to wear protection such as a full wetsuit or Lycra skinsuit.

  Treatment: in the event of a sting, the recommended treatment is to pour acetic acid (vinegar) over both animal and wounds and then to remove the animal with forceps or gloves. CPR (see page 103) may be required.

- **Scorpionfish** These are not considered dangerous in Mediterranean waters, but care should be taken against the spines on top of the dorsal fin.

  Treatment: inadvertent stinging can be helped by bathing the affected area in hot water. Any septic wound needs to be treated with antibiotics.

- **Sea urchins** The spines of some sea urchins are poisonous and all sea urchin spines can puncture the skin, even through gloves, and break off, leaving painful wounds that often go septic.

  Treatment: for bad cases bathe the affected part of the body in very hot water. This softens the spines, making it easier for the body to reject them. Soothing creams or a magnesium sulphate compress will help reduce the pain. Septic wounds need to be treated with antibiotics.

- **Stinging hydroids** Stinging hydroids often go unnoticed on wrecks, old anchor ropes and chains until you put your hand on them, when their nematocysts are fired into your skin. The wounds are not serious but they are very painful, and large blisters can be raised on sensitive skin, which can last for some time.

  Treatment: bathe the affected part in methylated spirit or vinegar (acetic acid). Local anaesthetic may be required to ease the pain, though antihistamine cream is usually enough.

- **Stinging plankton** You cannot see stinging plankton, and so cannot take evasive measures. If there are reports of any in the area, keep as much of your body covered as you can.

  Treatment: bathe the affected part in methylated spirit or vinegar (acetic acid). Antihistamine cream is usually enough to ease the pain.

- **Stingrays** Stingrays vary considerably in size from a few centimetres to several metres across. The sting consists of one or more spines on top of the tail; although these point backward they can sting in any direction. The rays thrash out and sting when they are trodden on or caught. The wounds may be large and severely lacerated.
  Treatment: clean the wound and remove any spines. Bathe or immerse in very hot water and apply a local

anaesthetic if one is available; follow up with antibiotics and anti-tetanus.

- **Weaverfish** These small fish like to hide just under the fine sandy surface in shallow waters. They have a sharp spine on top of the forward dorsal fin and many swimmers and snorkellers have been speared by stepping on one. Protective footwear should be worn at all times when entering the water.

  Treatment: for bad cases bathe the affected part of the body in very hot water. This softens the spine, making it easier for the body to reject it. Soothing creams or a magnesium sulphate compress will help reduce the pain. Septic wounds need to be treated with antibiotics.

- **Other stinging creatures**
  Venoms can also occur in soft corals and the nudibranchs that feed on stinging hydroids. If you have sensitive skin, do not touch any of them.

Cuts

Underwater cuts and scrapes, especially those caused by coral, barnacles and sharp metal, will usually, if they are not cleaned out and treated quickly, go septic; absorption of the resulting poisons into the body can cause more serious medical conditions.

After every dive, clean and disinfect any wounds, no matter how small. Larger wounds will often refuse to heal unless you stay out of seawater for a couple of days. Surgeonfish have sharp fins on each side of the caudal peduncle; they use these when lashing out at other fish with a sweep of the tail, and they occasionally use them to defend their territory against a trespassing diver. Their 'scalpels' may be covered in toxic mucus, so wounds must be cleaned and treated with antibiotic cream.

As a preventive measure against cuts in general, the golden rule is: do not touch. Be sure to learn good buoyancy control so that you can avoid touching anything unnecessarily.

Bibliography

Aquilina, Simon: *Treasures of the Maltese Waters* (1995), Aquilina Enterprises Ltd, Malta.

Campbell, A.C.: *The Hamlyn Guide to the Seashore and Shallow Seas of Britain and Europe* (1979), Hamlyn Publishing Group, London.

Cauchi, Achilles: *Dwejra* (1982), Gozo Press, Gozo, Malta.

Debelius, Helmut: *Mediterranean and Atlantic Fish Guide*, Ikan-Unterwasserarchiv.

Galea, M.: *Meldives Dive Booklet* (1995), Meldives, Malta.

Globetrotter Travel Map of Malta (1996), New Holland Publishers, London.

Göthel, Helmut: *Farbatlas Mittelmeer farma Niedre Tiere und Fische* (1992), Ulmer, Stuttgart.

Lanfranco, Guido G.: *The Fish Around Malta* (1996), Progress Press Ltd, Malta.

Malta, A Guide to the Islands' Heritage, National Tourism Organization, Malta.

Middleton, Ned: *Maltese Islands Diving Guide* (1997), Swan Hill Press.

Mojetta, Angelo: *Mediterranean Sea Guide to the Underwater Life* (1996), Swan Hill Press.

Richards, Brian: *Globetrotter Travel Guide to Malta* (1996), New Holland Publishers, London.

Sammut, Anton: *Diving the Maltese Islands* (1986), Submarine Exploration and Archaeology Interprint, Malta.

Index